DEVIL SICKNESS AND DEVIL SONGS

SMITHSONIAN SERIES IN ETHNOGRAPHIC INQUIRY

William L. Merrill and Ivan Karp, Series Editors

Ethnography as fieldwork, analysis, and literary form is the distinguishing feature of modern anthropology. Guided by the assumption that anthropological theory and ethnography are inextricably linked, this series is devoted to exploring the ethnographic enterprise.

Advisory Board

Richard Bauman (Indiana University), Gerald Berreman (University of California, Berkeley), James Boon (Princeton University), Stephen Gudeman (University of Minnesota), Shirley Lindenbaum (City University of New York), George Marcus (Rice University), David Parkin (Oxford University), Renato Rosaldo (Stanford University), and Norman Whitten (University of Illinois)

DEVIL SICKNESS AND DEVIL SONGS

TOHONO O'ODHAM POETICS

DAVID L. KOZAK AND DAVID I. LOPEZ

SMITHSONIAN INSTITUTION PRESS
WASHINGTON AND LONDON

Grateful acknowledgment is made for permission to reprint excerpts from the following copyrighted works: From *Cycles of Conquest* by Edward H. Spicer, copyright © 1962 The Arizona Board of Regents, published by the University of Arizona Press. From *The Pima Indians* by Frank Russell, copyright © 1975 The Arizona Board of Regents, published by the University of Arizona Press. From *Piman Shamanism and Staying Sickness* by Donald Bahr et al., copyright ©1974 The Arizona Board of Regents, published by the University of Arizona Press. "The Papago Cattle Economy: Implications for Economic and Community Development in Arid Lands," by Rolf W. Bauer, from *Food, Fiber, and the Arid Lands,* edited by William G. McGinnies et al., copyright © 1971 The Arizona Board of Regents, published by the University of Arizona Press. From *Papago Indian Religion* by Ruth Underhill © 1946 Columbia University Press, reprinted with the permission of the publisher. From *Social Organization of the Papago Indians* by Ruth Underhill © 1939 Columbia University Press, reprinted with the permission of the publisher. From *The Desert People* by Alice Joseph, Rosamund Spicer, and Jane Chesky © 1949 The University of Chicago Press, reprinted with the permission of the publisher.

Copy editor: Tom Ireland
Production editor: Robert A. Poarch
Designer: Janice Wheeler

Library of Congress Cataloging-in-Publication Data

Kozak, David L.
Devil sickness and devil songs : Tohono O'odham poetics / David L. Kozak and David I. Lopez.
p. cm. — (Smithsonian series in ethnographic inquiry)
Includes bibliographical references.
ISBN 1-56098-910-6 (alk. paper)
1. Tohono O'odham Indians—Medicine. 2. Tohono O'odham Indians—Religion. 3. Songs, Tohono O'odham. 4. Tohono O'odham Indians—Cultural assimilation. I. Lopez, David I. II. Title. III. Series.
E99.P25K69 1999
610'.89'9745—dc21 99-25831

British Library Cataloguing-in-Publication Data is available

Manufactured in the United States of America
06 05 04 03 02 01 00 99 5 4 3 2 1

⊗ The paper used in this publication meets the minimum requirements of the American National Standard for Information Sciences—Permanence of Paper for Printed Library Materials ANSI Z39.48–1984.

THE WORLD IS WORSE OFF WITH THE PASSING
OF DAVID I. LOPEZ AND LYNDA A. PRITCHETT
IN THE PAST YEAR.
THIS BOOK IS DEDICATED TO THE MEMORIES OF
THEIR KIND AND GIVING SOULS.

Contents

Acknowledgments

There are numerous people we wish to acknowledge and thank for their selfless and generous contributions to this work. This book would not exist were it not for their gracious generosity and thoughtfulness. Together we thank Billy Antone, Adelaide Bahr, Daniel Benyshek, Albie Burke, Kristin Burke, John Chance, Dario Del Piccolo, Joseph Enos, Kathleen Fine-Dare, Esther Griswold, Geri Kozak, Jesse Kozak, Camillus Lopez, Connie Lopez, Dorothy Lopez, Philip Lopez, John Martin, James McDonald, the late Josiah Moore, Kathy Nadeau, Stephen Perkins, Kathleen Sands, the late David Santos, Alison Stratton, Delbert Thomas, Enoch Thomas, Rose Thomas, Cedric Torres, Teresa Underwood, Shearon Vaughn, Suzanne Wheeler–Del Piccolo, and Kathy Wullstein.

A special debt of gratitude is owed to Donald Bahr for his efforts at making this a more readable and accurate book. He spent countless hours over many years agonizing with us over its content, accuracy, and interpretation. His expertise in O'odham oral traditions and culture helped to make this work better in innumerable ways.

The encouragement and expertise offered by William Merrill and Bob Lockhart at the Smithsonian Institution Press is greatly appreciated.

We also appreciate the generous financial support of Sigma Xi, the Jacobs Research Funds, and the Arizona Historical Society.

We remain, however, solely responsible for any errors in translation, conceptualization, interpretation, and representation.

DEVIL SICKNESS AND DEVIL SONGS

Introduction

The Tohono O'odham (previously called Papago) live in the Sonoran Desert of southern Arizona and northern Sonora, Mexico. Approximately 20,000 United States O'odham[1] live on three spatially distinct but politically merged reservations: Gila Bend, San Xavier, and Sells. (The three send delegates to a common tribal council.) The material for this work comes primarily from Sells, the largest and the seat of the tribal government. The work is about one aspect of the O'odham shamanic healing system, an illness known as devil sickness *(jiawul mumkidag)*. Today devil sickness is perhaps the most commonly diagnosed staying-Indian-sickness *(ka:cim mumkidag)* on the Sells reservation. There are approximately forty staying sicknesses that afflict or have afflicted the O'odham, and such sicknesses are diagnosed and cured by shamans (diagnosticians) and ritual curers (singers). Staying sicknesses are caused by the mistreatment of or disrespect toward the spirit of an animal-person (e.g., deer, badger, bear, horse), bird-person (e.g., swallow, eagle, hawk), human (e.g., owl, saint, devil, prostitute), insect-person (e.g., fly, butterfly), and natural phenomenon–person (e.g., lightning, wind).[2]

One interesting aspect of the devil story lies in how the O'odham theory of sickness and cure was influenced by and merged with Catholicism and capitalism via missionization, pastoralism, and wage labor. It is a story of the dynamic creation of culture in the New World. When viewed in historical perspective and cultural context, it is clear that devil sickness is much more than cultural exotica. Devil sickness and "way" (*himdag,* which translates loosely as "tradition"), part of O'odham shamanism and worldview, were influenced by Spanish, Mexican, and then American Catholic missionization on the one hand, and the

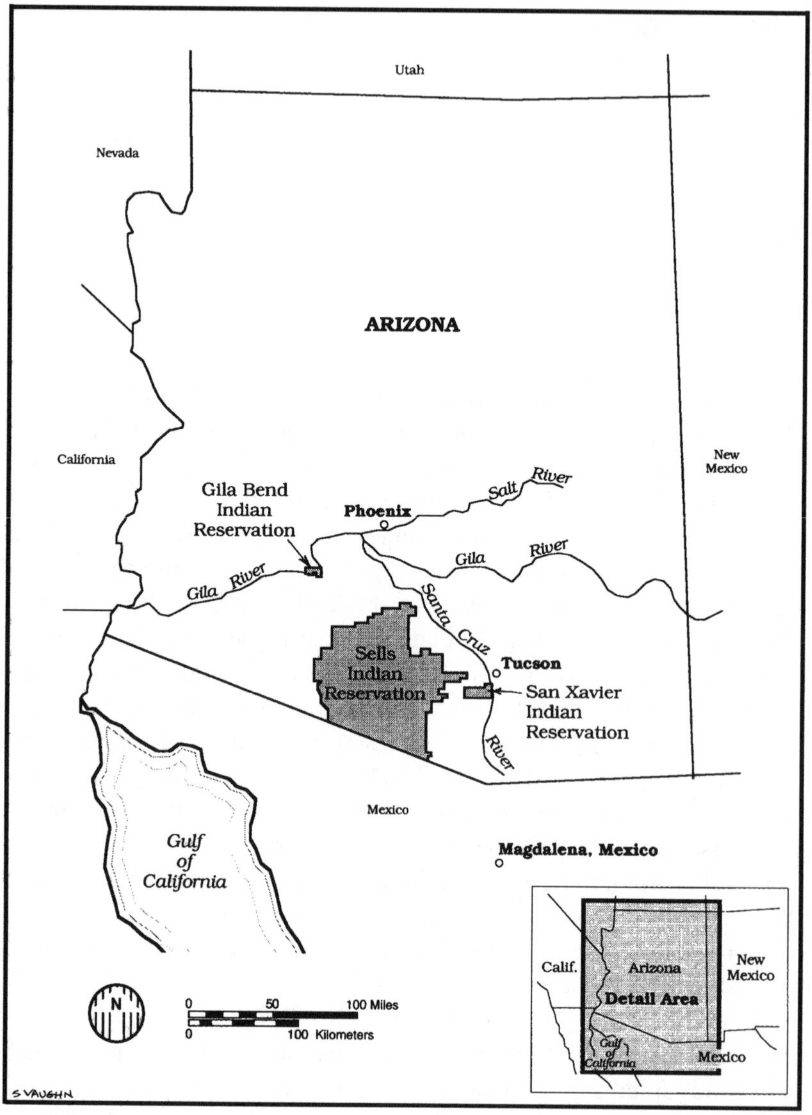

The Tohono O'odham reservation.

regional development of the Southwest cattle industry during the late nineteenth century on the other. It is a psychological, ideological, and material complex.

O'odham speak of their homelands as the staying earth *(ka:cim jewed)*. Numerous small mountain ranges border sweeping alluvial valleys in the starkly beautiful topography of the Sonoran Desert. Native plant life is dominated by numerous species of cacti, grasses, and mesquite and palo verde trees. The photogenic saguaro cactus is this desert's identifier plant. Rainfall averages between three and ten inches per year and falls primarily during two seasons, winter and summer. The gentle winter rains give way to the explosively violent summer monsoons. For the Tohono O'odham of the Sells reservation, no perennial streams or rivers flow through this landscape. A raging torrent in an arroyo one day may disappear entirely the next.

The staying earth is more than physical geography, plant life, or precipitation patterns. Sacred mountains, hills, springs, and shrines loom large in the O'odham imagination. Mythical accounts of origin, ritual orations, song poetry, and family stories refer to specific mountains, for instance, from where the winds emerge, where mythic heros encountered hardship, and where deities and spirits continue to reside. The staying earth is both sacred and profane and delineates the perceptual and physical boundaries of their universe.

Devils are prominent residents in this landscape. They make their homes in the interior of mountains—in caves or mountains said to be hollow—that dot the desert, usually near currently inhabited villages. Devil spirits, like their human cowboy counterparts, traverse the desert floor because they too are cowboys who love their job of riding horses, chasing and roping cattle, and the camaraderie with other devil cowboys. Because of the devil's close proximity to humans, the two come into frequent contact and interaction. This interaction can be beneficial, as when a devil gives a human the power to cure devil sickness or become an expert horseman or calf roper. But the interaction can also be harmful to humans when the devils protect their earthly property—livestock. Like all O'odham spirits who oversee their earthly charges, devils, in their case, protect horses and cattle. Devil sickness is the result of human misbehavior toward the devil's property. In addition, devils give deserving humans the ability to diagnose and cure the sickness that they cause. Devils and devil sickness, then, do not equate with the Christian belief of the devil as a quintessentially evil being. To the contrary, devils in the O'odham way of thinking are potentially good or bad, or often simply indifferent toward humans. Devils are some of the O'odham's ancestors: they are deceased O'odham cowboys. How devils act toward the living depends largely on human behavior toward horses and cattle. As with all spirit ways, it is simply a matter of respect.

Devil sickness is unique in the O'odham theory of sickness and cure because it blends indigenous and Christian cosmologies and because it is related to the development of the late nineteenth-century cattle industry in this part of the Southwest. Saint *(sa:nto)* sickness *(mumkidag)* is another blended sickness because it merges indigenous and Christian concepts, but saint sickness is not linked to cattle capitalism. The history of devil sickness blending, therefore, is important for shedding light on how the O'odham conceived of changes in their way of life from the late nineteenth century to the present.

Devil songs and devil-lore comprise the data for this book. Devil songs, like all O'odham curing songs, have an ancient source in that devils, the songs' authors, are conceived of as mythical beings, or at the very least they continue to reside in mythic time and place. When a human hears a devil song from a devil spirit, it suggests that the human was escorted back in time. Devil-lore is pervasive in O'odham culture. In addition to devil songs, we will consider the stories that circulate about devil spirits.

To tell this history we use a method of collaboration wherein a native person and a non-native person maintain their own voice in the text, so that their individual contributions and understandings are kept personal. When those first-person singulars merge into a "we," it indicates our agreement and shared understanding of the story. We believe that this rhetorical practice is essential for fully conveying our thoughts. It is our intent to offer a modest alternative to the common representational asymmetry found in some ethnographic literature. In our view, collaborative writing begins to level the literary ground for multicultural communication. Thus, the "I's" and "we's" are a representation of multicultural conversation or bridging dialogue. The story is based on devil songs (texts) and oral traditions (narratives) about devil way. In this manner the voices of others—singers, storytellers, and the devils themselves—will also be heard. This is both our method and theory of developing an anthropological practice of multicultural, politically symmetrical scholarship.

In addition to our conceptualizations on audience and text production, theorizing will take two paths. First, we use political economy to analyze devil-lore, the popular stories that circulate about devils. We justify its use on the basis of devil-lore content, which presents such themes as envy, jealousy, sorcery, and wealthy ranchers, but also gender relations. Devil stories reveal a hostility between the wealthy and the poor. From a materialist stance, the invocation of devils to explain wealth disparities symbolizes the impropriety, even immorality, that is suspected of the rich person. With a growing body of devil research scholarship in the New World, we evaluate a political-economy perspective by comparing the O'odham evidence to other research.

Second, we came to realize that the political-economy orientation was too limited for all of our conceptual needs. To analyze devil songs, we had to forgo making a political-economic argument. The songs simply do not provide the evidence necessary to sustain a materialist argument throughout the book. Instead, we theorize that the two devil song-sets we analyze possess what we call primary and secondary poetic tensions. The primary tension establishes the song-set's characters and their activities by describing events and scenes. The conceptually more important secondary poetic tension presents the listener with a philosophical question or dilemma early in the song-set that asks the listener (patient or other audience) to contemplate and resolve. This secondary tension is analogous to Lévi-Strauss's (1967) famous hypothesis on "abreaction"—the allegorical connection made between shaman and patient. The patient is invited to live or experience vicariously what the shaman or curer experiences in his or her shamanic dream-journeys. Through the vicarious experience, an abreaction is induced in the patient, thereby effecting a cure.

Finally, we wish to accomplish three general goals with this book: to present our theory of coauthorship in order to bridge the gap between native and non-native audiences; to describe and analyze devil way in O'odham culture in terms of its associations in shamanic tradition, Christianity, and cattle capitalism; and to present a theory of how O'odham song-poetic cures are structured and sequenced, and how this produces desired medical affects.

1

Writing about Devil Talk

Song-poetry is a special kind of language, an oral literature, esteemed in many Native American communities. Such poetry is sung in public ceremony, in private shamanic diagnosis and curing, in sharing drinks with friends, and when the singer is thoughtfully, reflectively alone. Song-poetic language is indispensable for the Tohono O'odham of southern Arizona, where song is a vibrant aspect of daily life in secular, sacred, and medical contexts.

O'odham think of song-poetry as a kind of ancient talk that originates in the normally unseen and mythical world of spirits. In their opinion humans do not compose this poetry, called *ñe'i.* Rather, humans hear the songs from spirits, the songs' authors, and they humbly memorize them. The continued vibrancy of songs lies in their ability to transform reality. Songs can make the rains fall, the sick well, and the sad happy. Song-poetry is a magical realism that is more real than magical. Because of its transformative qualities, song is central to the vitality, prosperity, and health of the O'odham community. It is a way for humans to make present the nonhuman, benevolent world of spirits, and it is a method for the spirits to reveal their presence to humans.

Devil songs *(jiawul ñeñe'i)*[1] are a genre of medicine song, of shamanic picture-poetry. They are sung by both shamans *(mamakai)* and ritual curers (*s-wusos o'odham,* literally, "blower people") in the diagnosis and cure of devil sickness.

O'odham respect these songs, like all medicine songs, for their diagnostic and curative properties as well as for their aesthetic and enigmatic qualities. They consider song to emanate from an ancient world and time that exists uncannily and simultaneously in the past and the present. One can say that song-poetry is a way to recognize a history that is both of the mythical past and continuously made palpable in the present. As an aesthetic verbal art, song-poetry can be admired as a divinely inspired literature for its terse, this-worldly, and riddlelike messages. As a necessary healing language, devil songs produce health and well being. And because devil sickness is today a frequently diagnosed staying *(ka:cim)* sickness, this healing characteristic cannot be overemphasized.

Devil songs, devil sickness, and the O'odham devil phenomenon, what O'odham call devil way *(jiawul himdag),* present anthropology, history, and the O'odham with a challenging fusion of Christianity and shamanism, of capitalism and a hunter-gatherer agricultural economy, that is, a fusion of distinct cultures. From an anthropological perspective, the O'odham devil figure and fusion occurred in a frontier context of conquest, colonialism, and neocolonialism. Devil songs and devil spirits provide unique insight into a process of social change, but a change that was mediated through traditional shamanic and cultural practices. Devils in this universe speak eloquently to pressures stemming from beyond the O'odham community's immediate influence, but pressures that demanded resolution in an O'odham manner. From an O'odham perspective, devils have existed from the beginning of the world; they have a mythical, not a historical genesis. They were created by I'itoi, the man-god creator of the O'odham people. Their presence is neither an academic mystery to be solved nor something that has a material foundation in economics.

O'odham devils often appear as phantasms to humans—as wealthy cattlemen or ranchers—but they also appear as ordinary cowboys. Wealthy devil cattlemen, wearing the finest and most expensive cowboy attire, are said to ride atop horses draped in silver-adorned halters and saddles. It is surely not the classic image of headdress-adorned Plains Indians riding bareback that we address here. Nor will we find O'odham devils in the Christian-folklore form of pitchfork-toting demons with crimson-colored skin, horns, and tail. Rather, the wealthy O'odham devil resembles Spanish missionaries and Spanish and Mexican *rancheros,* powerful and wealthy men of the cattle frontier. The wealthy devils possess large herds of cattle and horses. But devils are also described as ordinary cowboys, and in this case they are deceased O'odham who were cowboys during their lifetimes. Both the wealthy and ordinary devils' homes are nestled in various "hollow" mountains that dot the Sonoran desert landscape. From these homes devils imitate or communicate with the normal living human world. Inside the mountains are corrals and livestock, where roundups occur nightly, and where piles of gold and silver testify to the power and wealth of some devils. But devils are also identified with the horses that these spirit cowboys ride and with the cattle that they herd.

The devil spirit world mirrors the normal, day-to-day, human world, including the differences between the rich and the poor. Devils, spirit super-cowboys, are the spirit overseers of the late nineteenth-century frontier cattle industry, in which cowboy spirits control the important economic resources of cattle and horses. Devil songs, the primary method of communication between spirits and humans, primarily tell the story of the cowboy way of life, of the joys and freedoms of working on the range, but also, at least indirectly, of the economic transformation from an indigenous egalitarian way of life to one in which monetary exchange and commoditization became central.

Yet devil songs continue to speak, and emphasize, a more *traditional* language. They are, after all, diagnostic and curative texts used by shamans and ritual curers. Here, devil songs voice another kind of frontier, wherein Christianity has fused with the O'odham way.

The origins of devils and therefore of devil sickness is debatable. While, according to Kozak, it is not known and is unknowable whether devils and the devil phenomenon existed prior to the late seventeenth and early eighteenth centuries and European contact, but it seems unlikely. For one thing, devil songs and stories contain subjects that are historic references to the culture change that began for the O'odham around 1700. For instance, the devil spirit is a cowboy, not a traditional deer hunter or an owl (*cu:kuḍ,* deceased human spirit). For another, devil songs and stories are about cattle and horses, not deer or javelina (collared peccary); about excess wealth, not sharing and egalitarianism. According to Lopez, on the other hand, devils have always resided alongside of all the other spirits. Importantly, devil songs, like all medicine song-poems, are theorized to have an ancient or mythic origin and residence. Moreover, devils are thought to continue to reside in this mythic time-frame, like all other spirits. Our individual opinions on origins appear to be irreconcilable, because one hypothesizes a historical and secular origin, and the other a mythical and sacred origin. Donald Bahr (n.d., 1) provides a clue on how to evaluate this disagreement. Airplane songs are thought of by one O'odham shaman simultaneously as an anciently ordained and recently materialized phenomenon. For the shaman John Lewis, airplanes were imagined by the creator in the beginning, although never built by any O'odham. What is important to note is that while the material object, an airplane, was not physically or empirically present in the O'odham region until perhaps the 1930s or later, the spirit or way of it is rooted in the mythical past. From this we may draw the analogy that devils were imagined by the creator, but they did not materially appear in physical form until the Spaniards brought cattle and ranching into the region. Furthermore, since devils are some of their dead relatives, a link between ghosts *(cuckuḍ)* and devils was established. This analogy suggests that both of our perspectives have merit. Kozak argues for a materialist understanding, whereas Lopez argues for a spiritual one. While we disagree on origins, we feel this complements rather than detracts from our interpretations.

Methodologically and theoretically, this book is written as a multivocal text, wherein we each write from our own first-person perspectives as individuals, and also from a first-person-plural, collaborative, agreed-upon analytic perspective. We use both the O'odham and English languages, though there is an emphasis on the latter. Finally, there are the voices of the spirits, in song language. Those spirits form a third "I" voice in our narration. We translate and interpret two devil songsets or, in George Herzog's (1928) words, mythic dreamt song series, to show how devil song-poetry speaks words that extend far beyond their terse and elusive poetic realm and connect into political economy and ethnic history. Our primary interest is in song-poetry as a densely meaningful literature and in literature as an object of culture history. Thus, Kozak claims, and Lopez tolerates, that devil stories and to a lesser degree devil songs represent the O'odham's efforts to address the problems of money, Christianity, and their transformation from an egalitarian hunter-gatherer agricultural society to one grounded in pastoralism, wages, wealth accumulation, and monetary exchange.

To accomplish these goals and demonstrate our claims, we represent words with words, but words of special kinds—written from spoken usage, song, and words spoken in O'odham and English. They are words that belong to unique discourse communities: academic, indigenous, and other-worldly. This book is about bringing the words of special kinds, of unique communities, together into a conversation to make them accessible to divergent audiences in the service of working toward an egalitarian, multicultural communication.

Working Together

To emphasize our individual contributions, the two speakers, David Lopez and David Kozak, are identified by their initials.

DL: This man, this *milgan,* white man, named David Kozak, who I met some years back, asked if I wanted to do some Papago speeches with him. I told him that I'd find out from my wife Connie. Well, when she came home from work I asked her and she said that it's up to me to decide if I wanted to work with him. He said that if I didn't want to do these speeches then he would look for someone else. But he said that he really wanted me to be the one to do the speeches with him, and that he would pay me. So, after talking it over with my wife I told David that I'd go ahead and work on the speeches with him. We soon started running the tapes about the Papago language, tradition, and all that. We mostly talked about, and ran the tapes about, the devil sickness and all that is connected to that sickness. We also went around taking pictures of the mountains where devils live, and talked about the stories that I know about them—stories I have heard from long ago, and now, about our elders when they met devils in the mountains when they were on roundup. We also sang the devil songs that I know.

DK: I met David Lopez for the first time at his home in Covered Wells during the summer of 1988. At that time I was a master's student in anthropology, and my research was directed by Don Bahr. At the time I was researching violent mortality, traffic accidents, the commemoration of death, and cosmology. Don and I would occasionally drive around the Sells reservation, where he would introduce me to the people that he had worked with over the past thirty-plus years. We stopped at David's house, where we found him sitting in the shade outside of his home. Don and I had some beer with us, and we shared it with David. I didn't drink very much that day, and the two of them chided me about my teetotaling, and we laughed as they teasingly called me "the missionary."

> After our initial meeting, I didn't see David except at an occasional church or family gathering. Then, as I turned my attention to the O'odham devil phenomenon, Don suggested that I talk with David and determine if he wanted to work with me on my dissertation research.
>
> My initial interest in New World devil phenomena stemmed from a reading of June Nash's (1979) *We Eat the Mines and the Mines Eat Us,* and Michael Taussig's (1980) *The Devil and Commodity Fetishism in South America* as an undergraduate anthropology student. My exposure to religion stemmed from growing up in a conservative Lutheran family in Nebraska, and this contributed to my interest in how other people and cultures conceived of evil and the devil. After learning that the O'odham possess a lively devil song-poetic and folklore tradition, I was excited to learn of the significance and place of devils in O'odham culture and history. I wondered to what extent my findings would parallel or diverge from Nash's and Taussig's.
>
> In 1992 I went to Santa Rosa, where David Lopez and his wife Connie had moved. I told David what I wanted to learn about, and that I had a grant to support the research, and I requested that he teach me what he knew about devil sickness, O'odham cowboy culture, and song-poetry.

In August 1992 Kozak approached Lopez with a research plan and formally requested Lopez's participation. Lopez was very interested in the project and eventually agreed to participate. For two years we discussed, taped, and transcribed the complexities of devil way. Many of the bilingual texts of O'odham and English are the results of tape-recorded sessions in which Kozak asked Lopez questions about devil way, and Lopez responded with narration and analysis about devil way as he understands it. Lopez's narrations express his personal faith in the O'odham theory of sickness and cure, and they also speak to the cultural and historical milieu of which devil way is a part. Both of us spoke with other O'odham about devil way.

We worked together to plan and structure the order of his taped narratives, and to transcribe and translate them. Taping sessions occurred between August 1992 and December 1993. In May 1993 we began transcribing and translating Lopez's taped performances, what he calls "my little speeches" *(ṣo'oṣpolk ñ-ñeok),* and what Kozak calls didactic essays.[2] In addition to the taped narratives, we retranslated a set of four "demon" songs published in Frank Russell's *The Pima Indians* (1908, 329–30). Last, we collaborated in the translation and analysis of a set of thirty-five devil songs sung by the now deceased ritual curer, Jose Manol. These songs were recorded by Donald Bahr in July 1977.

After discussing our options, we decided that a question and answer format would best serve our purposes. We selected this format because devil orations do not exist as a distinct O'odham oral genre. That is, devil-lore is not codified in ritual oratory or mythology prose. Therefore, the question-answer format assisted Lopez in framing his thoughts and analyses. Questions were open-ended and posed in both English and O'odham by Kozak. For instance, a question could be posed as, "What is devil sickness?" or, "K hascu o wuḍ jiawul mumkidag?" Responses were at times in English, at others in O'odham.

The final textual organization and editing were left largely to Kozak, although we continually discussed the composition process as well. For instance, while working through the differences between devils *(jejawul)* and devil-owls *(jiawul cuckuḍ),* Kozak asked Lopez to evaluate Kozak's grasp of the material. Kozak explained to Lopez how he understood the differences, and Lopez would then confirm or critique Kozak's explanation. The present writing, then, reflects that kind of verbal exchange and editing.

Although a collaborative enterprise, our personal reasons for getting the story down on paper differed. We both believed, nonetheless, that describing devil sickness and the overall devil phenomenon would be important and interesting for several reasons. First, we felt that working together as equals was the preferred way of representing cultural knowledge.[3] We both believed that we had something unique and valuable to say about devil way, and to preserve our distinct voices, we decided to write in a manner that maintained and respected this individual distinctiveness. This method respects in writing the personal boundaries, and their permeability, implicit in any conversation.

Second, to best present our voices and our unique contributions as individual authors, we both write using first-person, "I," language. Texts written in the first person present our uniquely situated and personal perspectives, knowledge, experiences, and interpretations. But we also write, as here, in a first-person-plural, "we," voice. This presents our efforts toward a collaborative dialogue, a way to make statements that we both feel confident enough to agree upon. But it is also here that our merged voices serve to illustrate the very real and important practice of producing multicultural exchanges in a democratic, productive, and egalitarian manner.[4] It is here that personal boundaries are crossed. Still other voices enter into this work. These voices, be they from academically published sources or from previously taped or published song-poems, were not available to give their consent. Our incorporation of these voices is a literary move that replicates how discussions are cumulative processes composed, arranged, and expressed from bits and pieces, fragments, of other people's words. And like all conversations, ours does not possess a distinct beginning or end. Conversations simply and modestly continue and develop an inertia of their own.

Third, we believe that our words should reach audiences beyond the conventional anthropological or academically informed ones. Thus, we write in both the O'odham and the English languages. Lopez's audience is primarily O'odham, youthful O'odham, those who, according to him, know little of the traditions because they are being overtaken by American pop culture. But Lopez was also attentive to the anthropological audience. Kozak's audience was primarily an academic, anthropological one. But he too writes with the intention of reaching beyond that typical community of readers. We will say more about this below.

We conceptualize our work together as a bridging dialogue, an ongoing conversation between a non-native anthropologist and a native critic. We ask questions, answer them, contest, debate, review, represent, interpret, and challenge each other's words. In this manner we work together toward the goal of accurate translation, interpretation, and representation even though our individual criteria and conclusions are sometimes at odds. We find that our individual criteria, though different in some respects, strengthen rather than weaken our findings and representations. But, of course, it is part of your job, as reader, to evaluate whether our representations and analyses are successful in conveying something of the devil phenomenon.

O'odham Verbal Arts Scholarship

The study of O'odham oral "literature" has a recent and relatively brief history. The study of oral "tradition" goes further back, approximately one hundred years. The difference that we draw between oral literature and oral tradition is significant and reflects disciplinary trends in anthropology, folklore, and history. The primary difference relates to the role of the native "informant." Native workers in the production of ethnographic texts are nearly invisible and muted in the history of the study of O'odham oral traditions. Though the so-called informants were essential to monograph production, who they were and what exactly they contributed to a study was rarely given more than a footnote of explanation. The representative power of the anthropologist loomed large and submerged the efforts of native contributors.

Recent scholarship has shifted toward a recognition of the efforts of native anthropologists in the production of ethnographic texts that deal explicitly with O'odham oral literature. Unfortunately for us all, the informants of earlier days can no longer speak to us, and the record of their passing is spotty at best. The contributions of Jose Lewis Brennan, Juan Dolores, and Hawk Flying, among others, are virtually unknown when compared to what is known of the white ethnologists of O'odham, Frank Russell and Ruth Underhill.

Collaborative work in O'odham oral literature has a more recent history. Donald Bahr has committed himself to collaborative scholarship for approximately twenty years. In comparison to previous O'odham contributors, we know a significant amount about the men that Bahr has worked with over the past thirty years: Juan Gregorio, Baptisto Lopez, Jose Manol, and John Lewis.

DL: I grew up under my grandfather Juan Diaz Lopez, not my father, and I remember when he used to tell me about his life. I was about ten years old when he adopted me, and he showed me how to do ranch jobs like plowing fields, riding horses, and working as a cowboy. My grandpa was a medicine man, and he would take me with him when he went to cure people. I learned a lot from him. At fifteen I was shipped to Fort Apache to go to school. I guess that it was then that I knew that I was interested in anthropology and linguistics. I would ask my Apache friends lots of things about their culture and language. I asked what different things mean, and they would tell me. They told me about dangerous things like medicine man's tools and the things that they are superstitious about. So it is from that, my grandpa and my time at Fort Apache, that I started to find out that I enjoyed doing this, becoming an anthropologist. Like now, the Yaquis teach me about their language, and they tell me about their culture.

It was long ago that this man named Don Bahr started coming around from Massachusetts, and he stayed in the church and feast house one time. I remember that he really liked to eat rattlesnakes and he killed them and put them in the refrigerator in the community building. The people got after him because rattlesnake meat stinks. So a lot of the people began to know him, although I hadn't met him yet.

Another year he came around again, with his wife Dili, she's from Italy. They stayed at the late Jose Pancho's house, where they gave them a little crackerjack room. They were cold and were just sleeping on the dirt floor, and they didn't have any firewood to burn. They had their little daughter Maria Pia with them then. That is when I met Don for the first time, and we started going around to different places like Ge Hu'a Wai and Ventana Cave. He asked me if I wanted to do tapes with him, and I agreed. We started taping Juan Gregorio's speeches. And I translated his words the best that I could.

Don became good friends with the Papago because he speaks Papago. So that's when we got to know each other, and that's when I began working with him.

I went to Arizona State University, where Don got a teaching job. He bought a little house near campus, and I stayed there when I started translating the tapes of the late Juan Gregorio (Bahr et al. 1974). I ran big wheels of tapes, and it was my job to learn them. And I did Ruth Underhill's (Underhill et al. 1979) tapes too. I corrected the mistakes. I also worked on Juan Dolores's and Jose Lewis Brennan's. The talks were pretty good, but the writing was kind of hard to read. So I started doing this kind of work, doing the tapes and correcting them.

I met Ruth Underhill a couple of times. Papagos around here know her because she was a teacher over here, and this is where she first started doing anthropology, writing books. But some of her spellings are not too good because they sound like the *milgan*'s tongue, so I corrected them in the Papago tongue.

Ruth Underhill came several times when I was living at the

school. One time she came, and Baptisto, my father, and her sang some songs, and they were happy to see each other again. This man Joe Enos from Chui Chu took pictures, and they made a video, and the Papago's honored her for her writings.

So this is how I started doing anthropology and linguistics. I did a lot of the tapes with Juan Gregorio. He uses the Papago tongue in the right way, and at times I didn't understand him. I would ask him what he meant, and he'd just laugh at me and say, "Well, this is what we say. You speak Papago, but you don't really say it the right way." So he would teach me, and I learned from that. That's what I did with Bahr when he was running the tapes. I would try to jog myself to really do the best that I could to get the words straight, how Juan Gregorio would say things, and I would translate and interpret that into English. I would try to catch the way he said things in Papago so I could translate them into English. Sometimes it was hard to catch what he said. And now with David Kozak, we are doing the same thing. So I have been an anthropologist for a long time, and I really like it.

DK: David Lopez's contribution to anthropological literature has gone relatively unrecognized. As an interpreter and analyst of O'odham language and culture he has not received the recognition that he deserves. As Clifford (1988) observed, Lopez's voice and specific contribution to the multiple-author book *Piman Shamanism and Staying Sickness* (Bahr et al. 1974) is opaque. This, despite the fact that his efforts were seminal in this book's compositional success. Similarly, *Rainhouse and Ocean* (Underhill et al. 1979) is a case where his labor can easily go unnoticed. It is truly remarkable and significant that he has now worked with three generations of anthropologists. This certainly must be a rare fact of anthropological research, yet one worth appreciation from the academic community.

O'odham oral-arts scholarship is rich though limited. The anthropologist Frank Russell (1908) was the first to document Piman oral literature, but, as we will discuss later, his efforts are flawed. This work does provide an important base line or starting point for analysis and comparison of myth texts and diagnostic and curative song-poetics. Russell's success was due in large part to his interpreter's—Jose Lewis Brennan—interest and ability in documenting the O'odham language. Since this early work, song analysis has held the interest of many anthropologists.

Francis Densmore (1929) devoted a volume to the documentation of 167 songs sung by Sivariano Garcia and translated by Henry Encinas, both of San Xavier. George Herzog (1936) compared Piman and Puebloan musical styles. Ruth Underhill's ethnographic work among the O'odham early led her to a consideration of the singular importance of song in ceremonialism. Her *Singing for Power* (1938b) and *Papago Indian Religion* (1946) devote a great deal of effort to the contextualizing of music. Other minor early works include those by Chesky (1943), Schinhan (1937), and Gunst (1930).

More recently, the work of Donald Bahr and Richard Haefer (1978) have contributed to an understanding of music in curing. Bahr (1983a) has proposed a method of analyzing O'odham song and examined various aspects of social dance music (Bahr 1986b), hunting songs (Bahr et al. 1979), and ocean songs (Bahr 1991a). I have analyzed a set of social dance songs (Kozak 1992). Ritual oratory has also been examined by Bahr (1975) and Underhill et al. (1979). Bahr et al. (1995, 1997) have published important analyses of O'odham mythology.

This growing literature demonstrates not only the lively literary tradition of O'odham culture, but also that the tradition remains viable.

Translation, or Talk about Talk

Writing and reading, perhaps all linguistic communication, are about translation. While we believe this to be true we don't think that just any reading or translation is equally valid or accurate. In other words, while any reading or representation is humanly possible or conceivable, this does not mean that all readings are equally correct. There are limits to which translation, interpretation, and reading can be pushed. This is because reliable interpretation of verbal or written communication across languages depends on accurate translation, that is, at least in our way of thinking, on staying as close to the original utterances as possible. A *good* interpretation is one that maintains the integrity of natively produced songs, speeches, or even ordinary talk. And we consider *poor* interpretations to be those that move away from native verbal productions.

We present an extended series of translations and offer our thoughts on these translations to tell a story, a history, about the devil in O'odham culture. We do not entertain the conceit that ours is the only or final reading, translation, and interpretation. For instance, there are few female voices in this work. We feel that this is a shortcoming and one that we wish others will remedy. We do, however, consider that our efforts are an honest and diligent attempt to say something meaningful about one aspect of the world.

In this book, we provide two kinds of translations from the O'odham language into English. On the one hand, we translate ordinary talk, and on the other, we translate song talk. The methods and results are sufficiently different to warrant separate explications. In both cases, we use the same orthography.

The O'odham language belongs to the Uto-Aztecan language family, and O'odham is spoken by approximately 20,000 people. It is related to other native Southwest languages such as Hopi, Tarahumara, and Yaqui, among others (Miller 1983). While debate exists over the exact number of O'odham dialects, we accept Hill's (1996) division of a "peripheral" and a "central" dialect system with the peripheral dialect subdividing into four distinct varieties and the central subdividing into several indistinct varieties. The O'odham language is comprised of twenty-nine different sounds. We present the orthography here because orthographies are often placed in front matter or back matter as if they don't matter. It is our wish that your reading of this book will include an attempt to learn the orthography and to put this knowledge into practice as you read the O'odham words that follow. The following is a list of O'odham consonants, vowels, and nonconsonants and vowels with English equivalents.

Consonants:
b as in *b*ig
c as in *ch*art
d as in *th*is
ḍ as in bu*t*
g as in pig
j as in *j*ob
k as in *k*it
l as in cur*l*
m as in *m*onth
n as in *n*od
ñ as in ca*ny*on

ŋ as in fi*n*ger
p as in *p*in
s as in *s*ip
ṣ as in *sh*ip
t as in *t*op

Vowels:
a: as in pod
e: as in cool, but with the lips spread instead of rounded
i: as in machi*n*e
o: as in bo*a*t
u: as in tool
The short vowels *a, e, i, o,* and *u* are the same, only shorter in duration.

Nonconsonants and Vowels:
h as in *h*eart
w as in *w*in
y as in *y*es
' as in oh-oh (glottal stop)

Diphthongs:
When two vowels occur in sequence, the first vowel is always stressed.
ai is similar to the *i* in b*i*te
ei has no English equivalent but is like *peine* in Spanish
oi is like *oy* in b*oy*
ui is like *ooey* in g*ooey*

Our work advanced in weekly and sometimes twice-weekly meetings at Lopez's home in Santa Rosa on the Sells reservation. We usually worked for about five hours at a sitting, taking short breaks about once an hour. After recording approximately twenty hours of discussions, we began the process of transcription and translation. Kozak transcribed all of the English texts verbatim. All O'odham texts were transcribed verbatim by both of us working together. The tapes were replayed clause by clause so that we could hear their content. Since Lopez could not write due to arthritis in his hands, he would repeat (dictate) to Kozak clause by clause what he had said on tape, and Kozak would then write down his words. Lopez edited his own tape-recorded words in this process. At nearly every point, Lopez made minor editorial changes to clarify his enunciations, but rarely did he substantially alter the content of his narratives. Kozak then made literal, or interlinear, translations utilizing his technical grasp of the O'odham language. A final step in the process was the establishment of a freely translated English version. Lopez had primary responsibility for this. His poor eyesight made it uncomfortable for him to read the texts on the printed page, so to facilitate this step of translation, and again working clause by clause, Kozak read back to Lopez in O'odham what he had dictated to Kozak in the previous step of translation. This provided Lopez with yet another opportunity to edit his work. In this step of translation, Lopez took more liberties with the English translations than in the previous step. We often discussed possible English word choices before deciding on what we deemed to be an accurate translation. We will present Lopez's O'odham language narratives in their verbatim O'odham and free-English forms.

Using this method, we retranslated a set of four "demon" (devil) songs (see chapter 4) sung by the Pima singer Wiṣag Woi'i (Hawk Flying) in 1902 for Frank Russell and the O'odham interpreter Jose Lewis Brennan (see Bahr 1975; Underhill et al. 1979). We were curious to know if Hawk Flying's songs were substantially different from Manol's, or Lopez's own, because they were recorded over seventy-five years apart. Since the devil songs presented in Russell (1908, 329–30) were not word-for-word translations and were written using unconventional spelling, random and inaccurate punctuation, and line divisions quite different from other collected texts, and because they were given excessively Victorian English translations, we found it necessary to retranslate the published Pima song language into everyday spoken O'odham before we could provide a new and, we think, more accurate English rendition.

A further collaboration occurred between us and Jose Manol, a now deceased ritual curer. A set of thirty-five devil curing songs sung by Manol was recorded in July 1977, but Bahr had not translated or analyzed this song-set, and he suggested that we include them in our work. We transcribed, translated, and interpreted this song-poetry using a similar yet different methodology. It was similar in that Kozak played each song individually, as many as four times, until Lopez felt that he understood the sung form. Lopez then quietly sang each song to fix it in his memory, and then he would help Kozak learn the song. Lopez then dictated the O'odham song language line by line. Kozak then read back to him what he had written down. Lopez, in turn, provided corrections and a literal English translation. Later, after mulling over each song's content and structure, Kozak provided a free English version.

The translation of O'odham song-poetry requires a different methodology than is used in the translation of ordinary speech. The difference is due to the morphemic and phonemic transformations that words undergo when used in song. For Manol's devil songs, we used

Bahr's (1983a) four-step method to transcribe and translate O'odham song onto paper. The first step involved the aligning of song beats (represented by vertical lines) with word syllables written directly below. We used this method because "like all known Papago songs, [they] are sung to a very steady beat" (Bahr 1983a, 172). For example:

| | |
Ka ci me is a three-beat, three-syllable word, while
| | |
Ki me is a three-beat, two-syllable word.

This first step fixes how the song is actually sung in the syllabic and metrical form. This method replicates the length that individual syllables are held. Because we are most interested in this song-set as literature, this is the extent to which rhythm is reproduced; musical notation is omitted entirely. This is not to say that tonal music is not important, only that we find song meanings most compelling for our explanatory purposes.

Song language is different from the language of ordinary or everyday O'odham speech. Song language is in fact linguistically formidable. It is thought by O'odham that each syllable is a part-word, and that each syllable is a distinct and meaningful unit of verbal communication. This means that there are no or very few vocables in O'odham song, since vocables of the Plains Indian sort are not considered "part-words" (see Powers 1992). In song language, vowels and consonants are different from those in vernacular O'odham. For instance, *yoimeta,* "wanders," is *oimeḍ* in everyday speech, and *sisiwoname,* "flame," "flash," or "shine," is *siwoḍ* in everyday speech. The linguistic differences make learning songs difficult, even for fluent native speakers. For example, during our initial attempts at transcribing the thirty-five devil songs of Jose Manol, Lopez could not fully understand twelve of the songs. Many of the twelve used words that Lopez referred to as "ancient," or at least the songs used words in unexpected ways, and so the song's meanings were somewhat elusive. Through sustained mulling, Lopez eventually understood all but one of the thirty-five songs. With this said, and due to the peculiarities of O'odham song, we must make clear that our translations are not perfect. This does not mean that we can know nothing of the songs, nor that our interpretations are intrinsically faulty. Rather, it reveals the limitations and difficulties of the translation of poetry. In learning a new song, the foremost concern is to get the words straight. For O'odham singers, exact memorization of lyric content is demanded because the lyrics are densely meaningful. Thus they are difficult to comprehend and even harder to translate. Exact memorization is demanded because this is how the spirits said the songs to the human recipients, and diagnostic and curative efficacy rests on exact recitation (Bahr et al. 1979).

After writing how songs are sung in the poetic song language, the second translation step was to obtain a literal O'odham translation derived from the precise song language. Lopez performed this task. After memorizing the lyrics, he arrived at a word-for-word O'odham translation. This step is written beneath the first step. The first two steps were in Lopez's literary control in that he dictated, and Kozak took dictation. The third step was a collaboration between us. We discussed all English words that might feasibly translate, and then we selected a sometimes free, sometimes literal translation that satisfied us both. This translation step, from literal O'odham to English, is not reproduced in the book.

Step four offers a free English translation. This step was in Kozak's hands, though Lopez made suggestions concerning clarity and accuracy. The free translations are in capital letters beneath the step-two rendition. Kozak attempted to stay as true to the original O'odham style (word order, grammar) and content (word choice) as possible. For instance, in song, verbs are frequently placed at the end of lines. In the English translations, Kozak replicated this structure where possible. He did, however, exercise some creative license in interpreting the songs. He did not want to say more than the original songs, but he did wish to present them as compellingly in English as they are in O'odham. Because of this, the free versions will read as slightly awkward if not unusual English poetry.

We found no identifiable or appreciable differences between Hawk Flying's and Jose Manol's devil songs. It is clear to us that both songsets stem from the same poetic and historic tradition. In both sets, subjects, objects, melodic structure, and line composition, including verb placement at the end of each line, all conformed to the same fundamental and identifiable music tradition.

DK: Reliable interpretations and representations can only stem from accurate, word-for-word translations. Such translations are the product of efforts that take seriously what and how things are actually said. While it is to some degree true that not all words and concepts translate perfectly from one language to another, I believe that most can be. Even with concepts and words most resistant to translation, it is possible to obtain workable definitions that are open to further informed contemplation. Translation for us was a slow, at times agonizing process that taxed both my own and Lopez's patience. I came to realize what David already knew—that the translation process was the best way to assure the quality of our later efforts at interpretation and representation. As we sat day after day, often in one-hundred-degree-plus temperatures, I assured myself that this labor was central to what Lopez calls "getting the words straight." It was simply doing what was demanded in a collaborative venture such as ours. And while I cannot say that it was always enjoyable, I experienced a sense of satisfaction and pleasure as we worked together toward our shared goals. I was convinced that we were doing something worthwhile, a conviction that I still maintain. Now, several years later and many miles distant, as I write these words, I can't help feeling a bit nostalgic over the intense camaraderie that we shared. In 1994 my wife Lynda Pritchett and I moved to Colorado, where I took a teaching position. David and Connie continued living in Santa Rosa until David's death on February 12, 1998. Lynda died on December 1, 1998.

DL: When we translate it is important to get the words straight. We have to start there. And because we, the Papago, say things in our own way, in our own dialects, not everyone will agree with how we translate. Like the translations we did with Jose Manol's songs, compared to our songs around here at Santa Rosa, the singers are saying the same things, but the songs change a little. So it's all related to dialect, other people's dialect—we say things different. So when Kozak and I translate, some people from other districts will say, "Oh, no, that's not right, that's wrong." But others will agree that it's right. I will just say that we Papago know our own regional stories, and we don't say them exactly the same. So, some people will disagree with our translations because they won't sound right. But what we are doing with this book, others from here in Santa Rosa will say, "Yeah, this is right."

This is the way that it goes. We judge ourselves, the Papagos. The Pimas do it different, but we talk the same language, we understand each other. But they might say about our book, "Oh, this is a little off." Anyway, they will still understand it and say, "But it's OK." And so others might like what we are doing even if it's a little off. Like I said before, others don't know about this devil way, and others haven't heard the songs, and some might say, "Well, I don't hear this kind of song, so I don't really know. I haven't heard about this, so I don't know what it is."

This is why I write down the songs, the way the singing is, what this old man Jose Manol sings that I understand. I write it down the way that he sings it even though he is not from around here, and it sounds a little different from our songs around here. I understand him, but it's a little different than what I know.

When I don't understand something in the tapes, I go to older people and ask what it means, and they straighten me up. That's what we do around here, we talk about things. And that's what we do in this book. We go to them and ask, "What does this mean, what does this talk about, what do they mean by this?" For instance, there are some of the devil mountains that I had heard about in songs and the stories about them, but I had not seen them. When it appears in the songs and I don't know about them, I ask the older people and they tell me why it is named like it is or why the song says what it says. So they straighten me up, and because of the older people, I don't think that there is too much wrong with this book. I just think that it is important to get the words straight because other Papago will read this.

Audience

Collaborative, multicultural authorship begins with and requires a serious awareness and consideration of audience. Collaboration demands that potential audiences be respected in the writing process. Audience has rarely been discussed in anthropological literature (see

Bahr 1975; Finnegan 1992; Sutton 1991), but it is gradually receiving attention. Since the concept of audience is multifaceted in this work, we find it necessary to offer our thoughts and concerns on it.

In today's reservation context, O'odham audiences are more likely to hear and see television, and to a lesser degree read writing, than to hear O'odham orations, myth tellings, songs, or prose storytelling. They are generally less involved in O'odham oral literatures than they were twenty years ago. For better or worse, mass media are enjoyed as much on the reservation as they are in the nearby cities of Phoenix and Tucson. It is not rash to say that TV and videotaped movies have done more to undermine traditional oral culture among the O'odham than any form of intentional assimilationist policy. Rather than sitting around one's elders and listening to stories and songs, many young people today sit around and watch televised programs that originate in Hollywood. The visual media arguably exerts the most coercive form of acculturative pressure in O'odham communities today.

Both of us had an idea of who our audiences would be. While Kozak writes for a generally, though not exclusively, non-native and native, university-educated population interested in Indian culture, Lopez writes for his own people and, in particular, for the younger generation, whom he views in his more pessimistic moods as pitifully ignorant of important O'odham history and traditions. And while he also finds the anthropological goal of writing about O'odham culture important, he believes that this goal is primarily a means of maintaining what is being forgotten through time. For Lopez writing is one way that he and like-minded native persons can assure that the young will maintain an understanding of their culture(s), even if they do not receive traditional training in the old ways. Being a coauthor of this book was important for Lopez because he believes that it can be used in O'odham reservation schools as a supplement to, or substitute for, oral training at home on devil sickness in particular and staying sickness in general. For Kozak coauthorship of this book was important because he believes that anthropological scholarship must somehow emphasize the voices of those whom anthropologists typically write about. For him, the multiplicity of voices comes close to replicating the anthropological method and, in so doing, celebrates the diversity of perspective that anthropology is uniquely qualified to offer to the world.

DL: From when we began until now, my reason for writing this book, my audience, is the young people. It's today's young people who don't know about our traditions. But older Papago might also like to read about what we write. And people from other races, milgans, Mexicans, and others, whoever wants to learn.

But it is really the young ones who don't know about all of this, and it's our young people who need to know about the traditions. Our ceremonies used to be fun, and nowadays it's just going down because people are forgetting. It's not like the Yaqui, who still do all of their culture. They go out and perform their culture, and it's still pretty strong. But around here we are just forgetting. That is why some elders say that this is the reason the desert over here is getting dry, because we aren't doing the rain ceremonials like we used to. We aren't doing our culture, and so it doesn't rain. So it's just going down, and I don't know what it's going to be like for others in the future.

You see, today the kids are just speaking English, and they don't use very much Papago anymore. It seems like they are just forgetting it or they are ashamed of it. But I also think that we forgot a lot of things because we didn't write them down.

I also write for other older Papago my age and older ones. They might be interested in reading about this because they don't know about devils, or they just know a little bit, and they might like to read about it. And then there are milgans and others that will want to learn about it, our way.

Like I said, the young people, while they know about devils because they are taught this in churches, they probably don't know that there are devils in the mountains. I want to tell the kids that there are devils around, to be careful. But like older Papago, like myself and others my age, and especially our elders, they know that devils are around here, although we don't see them unless they appear in our sleep or when we get sick. But our kids and little grandkids don't know that devils are around. They know there are devils because they heard about it from the Bible. But they don't know that there are really devils around here like ghosts' spirits and other animal spirits. So I think that they might be interested in finding out about this, our traditions.

DK: I write for an academic, primarily anthropological audience. But I also write for the O'odham community. I have found, as with many other anthropologists, that it is unacceptable for anthropologists to talk only amongst, to, or about ourselves or for others. If *we* as a community of speakers are to be relevant outside of our discipline, we must speak *with,* rather than simply *about,* the communities where we conduct our research. This means that we must rethink our invisible, taken-for-granted audience conventions, just as we have had to scrutinize our writing conventions.

Audience considerations are virtually nonexistent in the anthropological literature. In fact, if we wish to gain insight from an audience literature, we must go to rhetoricians and reader-response theorists (Ede and Lunsford 1984; Ong 1975; Park 1982; Said 1982).

Whereas representation and interpretation have been the subjects of theoretical debate (cf. Clifford 1986, 1988; Marcus 1986; and Marcus and Fischer 1986, among many others), audience has remained an unrecognized variable in the writing of ethnography. One need only examine the index of any ethnography to see the absence of and presumably the lack of concern for audience. This absence is particularly surprising given the extreme emphasis on literary experimentation and narrative development promoted by postmodern scholars, with their focus on experimental representation and critique of anthropology as social science. The emphasis on representation, at the expense of audience, has fostered, for one thing, a self-reflective, autobiographical posture. Here, the author-anthropologist has in some reportage become the focus of writing rather than who or what is ostensibly being written about, for, or to. And if the primary intent of anthropological research is to gain an understanding of or explain other histories and experiences, or promoting an appreciation of cultural difference, then this emphasis on autobiography is at least partly misguided. If we are also desirous of reaching nonacademic and native audiences, then our conventions—whether scientific or postmodern—need modification. Postmodern representations, like their scientific counterparts, are equally guilty of promoting what I call repre-

> sentational asymmetries. That is, who gets to say what about whom is grounded in the unequal access to political, economic, and educational power, and this is related to the inability to represent one's own culture (cf. Sponsel 1992). Representational asymmetries, whether scientific or postmodern, in my view, maintain, if not exacerbate, the divide between *us* and *them*. It perhaps widens the division between who writes and who is written about.
>
> To me, representational asymmetries are maintained in scientific accounts when the author takes the distanced, third-person, generalizing stance of social science, which tends to allow indigenous voices to be heard only in the capacity of an inert "data" source. Postmodern asymmetries stem from the distanced language of the literary critic and the emphasis on self to the avoidance of the Other in their quest to avoid making generalizations of any kind. In either case, both perpetuate asymmetrical representations of self and other (there are, of course, exceptions to both). For both writing strategies, the author maintains a textual control that allows little room for voices and audiences other than of the anthropologist's making.
>
> For me, to begin to close the divide, to diminish the representational asymmetries and move toward the democratization of text production and the promotion of multicultural communication, *us* and *them* need to be bridged in the practice and aims of anthropological writing. And this can be at least partly accomplished through the careful consideration and explication of audience-related concerns, and through coauthorship.

Throughout our collaboration, we each had the other's audience in mind. We were compelled to shift our literary allegiances numerous times in the translation and composition process to present the best possible content and form given our distinct backgrounds and intentions. This shifting occurred when we confronted O'odham words for which an exact English equivalent was unavailable. Then we debated how to best render the word or concept in English. Similar debates occurred over how to write various words in O'odham. Still other debates ensued when the limitations of the English language left us with no fully satisfactory linguistic substitute for an O'odham word or concept.

Audience has yet other meanings. Audience in the academic anthropological culture refers to persons who expect to see certain compositional features and rhetorical strategies (whether they are conscious of them or not). Variously, for example, hypotheses, citations of relevant publications, data, discussions of theoretical-conceptual matters, and explanations or interpretations are all characteristic of this audience's expectations. This audience generally includes academic or applied anthropologists, their students in college or university courses, and a few interested laypersons, mostly non-Indian, with a middle- or upper-middle-class background. Audience in O'odham culture may refer to humans, spirits, the living or nonliving. Song, orations, and prose storytellings all target different audiences. Songs in general are meant to carry the farthest to be heard by spirits, a curing song's most important audience. In fact, during curing sessions, it is technically—though not palliatively—unimportant that patients hear the songs sung for their cures. Songs are sung to please, even stimulate, the spirit-cause of the patient's sickness, and to be effective, voice must be confident and carry a long distance to the spirits who inhabit the ancient world as well as the present to the body of the patient. Ritual orations carry the next farthest and are meant for both humans and spirits. Prose storytelling carries the least distance, and such storytelling is meant solely for the ears of those people present at the telling (Bahr 1975, 5–8). It is this last kind of audience that now finds itself in front of a TV rather than in front of a grandparent.

With these audience distinctions in mind, we agree that Lopez's audience is not the spirits. Lopez does not address the supernatural landscape in his speeches or song critiques. He is not speaking words that spirits necessarily need or want to hear. Kozak was his immediate audience, although some of his grandchildren or his wife would listen in from time to time. Lopez's speechmaking was therefore unconventional in a traditional oral literary sense because it often stemmed from Kozak's direct queries. In this way his narratives are not of a prose storytelling sort generally associated with the recounting of tribal or family history. One might then logically ask: Where do Lopez's "speeches" or efforts fit into O'odham oral literature? We offer this answer: Lopez's words are the very personal and secular contemplations and theorizations upon a sacred topic. They are not in themselves sacred speech events. They are not part of a *traditional* literary practice because outside of song-poetry, devil-lore has not been codified into a series of prose texts or myths. Rather, we have come to regard Lopez's verbal essays as cultural critique.

Lopez critiques O'odham culture and literature when he reflects on and analyzes the meanings related to devils in O'odham culture. Though his essays are not *traditional* in any conventional sense of that term, his efforts as critic become highly relevant in a world flooded with stultifying and homogenizing mass media images and discourses.

2

History of Cattle, History of Devils

> **To a Papago a cow may represent a walking check book. . . . [I]f a man needs a hundred dollars for his family, or a fiesta, a funeral, or a marriage . . . he literally goes and cashes [in] one cow, or perhaps two or three cows. . . . He doesn't keep money in the bank. His bank's walking out on that reservation.**
> Charles Whitfield

From an anthropological and historical perspective, the history of cattle raising is synonymous with the history of the devil in O'odham society. For social science the two are inseparable in O'odham culture. Thus, to understand devil way as shamanic practice it is necessary to understand the economic culture history of cattle in the O'odham experience.

Cattle are not only central to O'odham economics, they are a way of life. Cattle and horses were introduced to the O'odham in the late seventeenth century by Jesuit missionaries. It was not, however, until the mid to late 1800s that livestock assumed their current importance for them. Between the 1700s and about 1880, O'odham hunted cattle much as they had hunted deer. It is not known how many O'odham men learned animal husbandry from the Spaniards, but it was probably relatively few. By 1900 beef replaced agricultural produce and wild game as the primary food staple. While some O'odham had early on learned ranching techniques and how to ride horses from the Spaniards and later from the Mexicans, their own cattle-raising efforts were aimed at its subsistence potential rather than sale on the market for profit. Subsistence cattle raising remains to this day an important source of food for a majority of O'odham families, whereas horses offer some prestige for O'odham cowboys and recreation for many more. Alongside the subsistence orientation, and beginning in the

1880s, a few O'odham men and their families grew large herds for sale in the burgeoning Southwest cattle market.

Livestock mark a profound change in the course of O'odham society. Although livestock had been known to the O'odham for nearly two centuries, cattle, horses, and other domesticated animals such as sheep, goats, and chickens remained peripheral to their subsistence-oriented economy. Geopolitical factors beyond the O'odham's territory and immediate political control had come to a turning point by 1870. Multiple factors, including, but not limited to, the end of the Civil War, the 1848 Treaty of Guadalupe Hidalgo, the Gadsden Purchase of 1854, the pacification of the Apache by the United States and their ultimate incarceration on reservations, and Anglo settlement in the Arizona Territory had direct and lasting consequences for all O'odham. The Sonoran Desert was primed for an influx of cattle that culminated in the establishment of a large cattle industry throughout Arizona.

By 1890 the O'odham practiced two general types of cattle husbandry. The first type, subsistence cattle raising, supplemented their primary subsistence work of hunting, gathering, and floodwater agriculture. First hunted like wild game, then herded, cattle were a dependable food source and later a source of supplemental cash. In the past, just as today, most but not all O'odham possessed at least one head of cattle and one or more horses. O'odham came to view cattle as a walking bank account, not unlike the way various Plains Indians viewed buffalo as a walking grocery. In the second type, commoditized cattle ranching, cattle were grown for the market, to be sold for profit in large numbers. This type was first established and is sustained in the southeastern portion of today's Sells reservation around the villages of Topawa and San Miguel. A few men who owned these large herds came to be known as "cattle kings." Commoditized cattle ranching created a social division that was based, for the first time, on control and access of economic resources rather than on control and access to supernatural power. Prestige, for some, came to be counted and defined in the number of cattle and horses one possessed.

DL: Individual people own cattle and horses. Cattle are used for many things. Like at times they are used for celebrations, or for death anniversaries, or for a death in the family. They are also sold to make a living. Then again, when people go on the Magdalena pilgrimage they will sell their cows to get to Mexico and to buy things that they need. People sell their cattle to get good things for themselves, their family, and for friends. We also have animals that we keep as our pets.

Way back, like I know that some people way back, and my late mom did this too, and my other relatives, they used to milk cows to make cheese. A lot of them did that. They would keep their cows and milk them to make cheese to sell, to make some money, and we used to like to drink fresh milk. Like over here at Santa Rosa, a few people used to keep a lot of cows. I'll say about fifteen head. And every morning, early in the morning, they would milk them. And my late Mom used to send us kids over there early in the morning—she'd give us a bucket, or some kind of jug, and we'd go over there and buy milk from them. And at times they would say, "Oh, we'll just give it to you for free, go ahead and take it."

We would use cows for special occasions, too. At times some people would say, "Oh, I baptized this child, I'll give her or him one of my cows." Godparents give cows to their godchildren. That's how kids start their own herd—it starts when their godparents give them one or two. If the godchild can afford it or, you know, if they can make it, they will keep the cow and start raising their own.

But some can't keep them because they want the money instead and so they sell them right away. They get rid of them. Some of them want to keep them and raise their own. But the extra money is pretty good, and when you are really broke and need the money, then you can sell maybe one or two to get money when you really need something.

But I think that some just waste their money. They shouldn't just play with it, shouldn't just think, "Oh, I need some money, I want to go here, I want to do this. I want to buy this because I know I have money in the cows." And here things are expensive.

Some of us will really try to make it, and will raise cows until we're really broke, and we really need money. And we'll just sell one or two at a time. And this is how we Papago have our cows. But some just play with them, they sell them right away. And here cattle are good, and at times when my late grandpa used to have cows, he would just butcher one, and people would buy meat from him. At other times he'd say on some special occasion, "I'll slaughter a cow and invite my friends to have a little celebration."

We also use cattle for our own use. We would kill one and make it into jerky and store it away, and eat it whenever we felt like it. And we know how to store it so it wouldn't get spoiled. We could eat it for months, or if we have some special holidays we get in little gatherings. We would invite close-by friends, family, or visitors who come by. So that was how my late grandpa kept his cows.

That is how we Papago like to raise and use our cows. We did that, and a lot of people still do now—those people who have a lot of cattle. At times they will just kill one to have other people come around to celebrate.

DK: In early October when the extreme summer temperatures abate, many O'odham pilgrimage to Magdalena, Sonora, Mexico, to the Church of Santa María Magdalena. The pilgrims celebrate their patron saint, Saint Francis Xavier. Most travel by car or truck today, whereas in the past the journey was made on horseback or in covered wagons. Some faithful who had asked for and obtained his divine intercession make the trip on foot to pay for the divine intervention. The first thing pilgrims do upon arrival in Magdalena is to line up for their turn at gently caressing, lifting the head of, and kissing the reclining image of the Saint Francis. [Lifting his head indicates that the person is in a state of grace.] Pilgrims bring gifts to and pin *milagros* on his image. They pray to him for good health, safety in their travels, good fortune, problem resolution, and happiness, among other things. O'odham pilgrims often bring their own personal saint images from their home altar or from roadside death markers, or they purchase new ones in Magdalena, to have them blessed and empowered by this saint. They place their saint against the reclining image of Saint Francis to recharge for another year the strength of their personal images.

As with most, if not all, Catholic pilgrimage sites, alongside the sacred activities is a carnival of profane diversions. The Magdalena pilgrimage is no different. All-night music, food, carnival rides, games, old and new friends, and alcohol make for a festive occasion. The small village of Magdalena is overrun with thousands of pilgrims and those who cater to them. Pilgrims camp in the backyards of local residents for a fee. It is amazing to see how many vehicles and people can be crammed into very small backyard spaces.

The pilgrimage costs money: gas for the vehicle, food, buying treats or more saint images, and enjoying the carnival that surrounds the church activities. It was and still is common for people to sell a head of cattle to finance the trip.

Aboriginal Subsistence Strategies

Discussed in the literature as Two Villagers[1] (Fontana 1983a), the Tohono O'odham are known, both before and after contact with Europeans, to have shifted their residence twice per year. During the winter months they lived in mountain foothills near permanent springs. Here the O'odham ate hunted and gathered foods. During the summer they moved to field villages to farm fields at the mouths of arroyos. Known as arroyo-mouth *(ak cin)* agriculture, this floodwater farming method depended on the fickle summer rains. Temporary rock dams and spreader brush dams were built to efficiently channel whatever runoff was available. Castetter and Bell (1942, 56) estimated that their agriculture of corn, beans, and squash accounted for 4 to 30 percent of their diet.[2] The relatively low percentage range is largely a result of the unpredictability of rain in this part of the desert.

Floodwater agriculture was risky due to the paucity and unreliability of rainfall (no perennial streams flow through the Sells reservation). The localized nature of the fierce summer monsoons made floodwater irrigation an unpredictable venture. Add to this the hazards of insects, severe and damaging rains, and animals, and O'odham agriculture was periodically a chancy mode of production. In response to these objective hazards, a field village consisted of extended-family compounds spaced unevenly and often a mile or more apart along several miles of wash. This type of decentralized settlement pattern is known as *ranchería* settlement and is a common economic strategy in the aboriginal Southwest.

Due to the climate, as with many other indigenous Southwest

peoples, O'odham worldview, cosmology, and ceremonialism revolved around securing sufficient rainfall. In fact, all O'odham ceremonialism, of both an individual and communal sort, had a hydrologic component. All agricultural efforts were mediated by a set of ideas based in human-environmental reciprocal interaction, especially those concerning water.

Hunting and gathering were also important in the O'odham subsistence economy. Deer, javelina, antelope, bighorn sheep, rabbits, quail, and rats were hunted according to availability. Gathered flora included several species of cactus—saguaro, cholla, prickly pear—and numerous species of green leafy plants and mesquite pods. The importance of these subsistence pursuits is attested to by the mythical and ceremonial beliefs and practices that offered guidance in both activities. For instance, deer hunters *(mo'obḍdam)* thanked the deer spirit *(huawi)* or gambled with the potential consequence that deer would not offer themselves to humans for killing and consumption (Underhill 1946, 101–15). Gathered saguaro cactus fruits also figured largely in the O'odham ceremonial cycle. A wine made from the sweet syrup of this fruit served a vital role in securing rain for their fields. This wine was consumed during the annual sit-and-drink ceremony, which was and continues to be conducted to ensure plentiful rainfall.

Cooperative economic practices were central to survival, and the O'odham's economic, social, and political organizations were all geared toward this end. Cooperative labor, gifting, and ownership stand out as good examples. Cooperative labor consisted of neighbors who worked together to construct brush check dams and plant, weed, and harvest each others' fields. And even though one's own field may be unproductive one season due to some natural constraint, a neighbor's field a mile away may turn out to be very productive. By sharing labor a family reduced its dependence on its own fields in that one's neighbors could be counted upon to provide extra food during lean times. Bahr (1983b, 190) put the relationship this way: "By helping different households in widely scattered locations, and by being helped by them at each stage of the farming process, each household's fields became a well-cushioned bet against the risks of Papago agriculture."

Gifting was important as well. Gifting was a form of generalized reciprocity whereby an object was given without expectation of immediate return. Whether the gift was food, a horse, or a tool, the giver gave with the expectation that a return would be made at some unspecified future time. A giver gave because it was advisable to dispose of surpluses while still palatable and thus invest in social good-will. Nor was the amount or the kind of the gift return specified. Gift exchange, like cooperative labor, acted to buffer lean times, and it was hoped that the one who had initiated such an exchange would have something to fall back upon if they had trouble obtaining enough food to get by.[3] Both cooperative labor and gifting served as an insurance policy of sorts against the unpredictability of the desert (Underhill 1939).

Food is a particularly good example of cooperation. The sharing of food is a profoundly important practice in all human cultures. From an infant's bonding to its mother and until death, food is nourishment for both the physiological body and the cultural body (Mintz 1996). What is considered good to eat is largely a matter of culture, and its exchange carries a rich symbolic load. For O'odham who inhabited an occasionally food-scarce environment, the need to nourish the physical body led to cultural body practices ensuring that individuals could satisfy that need. The circulation of food was never ending. Even during times of plenty, food gifts to neighbors and relatives maintained ties of mutual responsibility and care. One's connection to and acceptance by the group was mediated by and symbolized with food along with its creation and the generation of what Bourdieu (1984, 291) calls "symbolic capital." Surplus food, for example, was given away as gifts because value never accrued with the accumulation of goods; rather, value—symbolic value—accrued with its dispersal to others.

The concept of ownership, while it existed, seems to have been limited. This is not surprising, because the development of surpluses and possessive self-interest in O'odham communities would be antithetical to gifting and cooperative practices. Families owned very little permanent or inalienable property. While extended families generally possessed use rights to fields for agriculture, and saguaro cactus groves and collection areas for gathering, which were recognized publicly, this "ownership" was considered alienable, and what's more, landowners usually allowed others access to it for the asking.

Individuals owned personal property such as clothing, tools, weapons, and ceremonial equipment, but anything one could acquire could also change hands. Linguistically, the suffix "*-ga*" is added to nouns of objects that are both acquirable and alienable (see Bahr 1986a).

Horses, cattle, autos, and money are examples of alienable commodities. Such things as one's own body, emotions, thoughts, and blood relatives, while "possessed," are not alienable to a person and therefore are never suffixed with "*-ga*." This linguistic form embeds the ephemerality of the ownership principle and experience in O'odham culture.

It was not until the late nineteenth century that the concept of personal ownership took on its current connotation. The development of the livestock industry and wage labor fostered the notion of possessive, accumulative self-interest. By 1900, and thanks in part to brands for cattle and horses, the cash economy, and wage labor, O'odham ownership practices emulated Anglo and Mexican forms. It is still true, in an altered form, that gifting and ownership principles reflect norms and values extant one hundred years ago.

O'odham political leadership reflected the fluidity of these economic and social arrangements. Consensus rather than decree, and old age and experience rather than youth and precocity, marked O'odham political life. Each *ranchería* community had its own autonomous council of elder males. These men discussed and decided upon such matters as agricultural works, hunts, warfare, dates of ceremonies, and intervillage games and socials. There were no formalized governmental institutions, nor was there a network that linked the separate *rancherías* into a single unified tribal polity. The Tohono O'odham "tribe" is a federal invention of the United States. War leaders and shamans were distinct individuals with some individual political power, yet authority depended largely on village consent. And without hereditary political offices, authority was diffuse. The diffuseness of O'odham political organization reflected the necessity of individuals and families to respond as needed to environmental and social constraints. The upshot was that extended families maintained control over the decisions that directly affected them. Each family decided for itself what it would do at any given moment (Underhill 1939).

Aboriginal O'odham subsistence practices consisted of a system based on extended-family and intracommunity sharing. It was an economics tied closely to bonds of kinship in a decentralized political structure that was sanctioned by a mythico-religious system that emphasized cooperation, equality, and environmental balance. Cooperation and equality of material wealth, with little by way of political and social hierarchy, assured that all had an equal share in the product of the community's labors. These social adaptations were perhaps necessary in an environment that was as unpredictable and potentially harsh as that of the Sonoran Desert.

The Southwest Cattle Industry

Europeans have tried to establish cattle ranching in southern Arizona within the past two hundred years. First the Spaniards, then the Mexicans, and finally the Americans are players in this history. With varying results, Europeans confronted similar problems on the frontier in their efforts to establish this industry. The Western Apache and Mescalero Apache Indians were perhaps the major early and persistent hindrance to its development. Apaches resisted the colonial efforts of Spaniards, Mexicans, and Americans with equal determination. They resisted reduction and encroachment on their land. Other factors such as the native *ranchería* settlement pattern, lack of funds, extreme climatic conditions, and competing military conflicts hampered the colonizers from successfully controlling the region. A successful ranching enterprise was not fully realized in southern Arizona until the 1880s, during U.S. occupation.

Conquest via mission building was the Spanish method for expansion into today's southern Arizona. First the Jesuits and then the Franciscans came with the desire of converting the so-called pagan populations of the region. Their strategy was to reduce the *ranchería* Indian settlements into compact, orderly communities with a Catholic church and plaza central to them. Livestock and plant domesticates assisted them in their efforts. At the front of early Jesuit efforts was Eusebio Kino, who supplied livestock to each of the twenty-five missions he founded in northern Sonora, Mexico, and southern Arizona to provide food for the missionaries and their Indian charges as well as support the missionary efforts in Baja, California. In 1700, for instance, he sent 700 cattle to the newly founded mission outpost of San Xavier del Bac near Tucson (Bolton 1932, 66).

Mineral wealth was discovered in the Southwest (largely in northern Sonora, Mexico) soon after the arrival of the Jesuit missionaries. Its discovery led to the settling of large *ranchos* (landed estates) by Spanish and Mexican colonists throughout the eighteenth and nineteenth centuries (Haskett 1935, 4–5). Although mining was the primary interest of the *rancheros* (ranch owners), they were compelled to raise livestock to supply food for themselves and their laborers. As various observers have noted, these early plantations were well stocked with livestock (Sheridan 1988; Wagoner 1952).

Soon after Mexico gained its independence from Spain, the Mexican military withdrew its protection of Mexican settlers in the northern reaches of its territory. Mexico had more pressing military matters to contend with in the Yaqui Indian resistance to the south. Due to a weak Mexican military presence in the region, the Apache intensified their raiding of European settlements and ranches, driving off livestock and occasionally killing or carrying into captivity some of the ranchers. Eventually, the *ranchos* were abandoned (Haskett 1935, 7). The quick exodus of Europeans from the region meant that the majority of their vast cattle herds were often simply abandoned to fend for themselves. The herds reverted to a semiwild state, and numerous reports tell of vast and at times aggressive wild herds. The Mormon Battalion, for instance, encountered them in droves. These militiamen killed the cattle for food, and it is reported that aggressive bulls were a constant physical threat to the troops (Beiber 1938, 143; Williams 1916, 6). The Apache also hunted these cattle as a food source, while professional cattle hunters from Mexico made hunting expeditions into the region to harvest meat and hides (Beiber 1938, 194; Haskett 1935, 9).

Beginning in the 1850s, the first cattle introduced in the region from the United States arrived via cattle drives from New Mexico and Texas. The gold rush to California brought many emigrants through southern Arizona on their way to fulfilling their dreams of quick wealth. The Texas-to-California cattle drives supplied food for that growing and hungry population, and they were targets of Apache raids. And although the Gadsden Purchase of 1854[4] transferred possession of the region to the United States, this did not translate into an immediate cessation of Apache raids. The Civil War drew most of the Union soldiers and equipment back East, thereby leaving emigrants in the Arizona Territory vulnerable. It was not until the late 1860s that U.S. troops returned in numbers large enough to quell the raiding and eventually incarcerate the Apache on reservations. Incarcerations of Apache and of other western Indians on reservations, in addition to the military occupation of the region, created an extensive Arizona cattle market. The troops and those Indians placed on rations had to be fed.

Apache resistance gradually diminished throughout the 1870s, and social and political conditions, for the first time, were amenable to uninterrupted cattle production. In 1870 there were only 5,000 cattle in the Arizona Territory, but their numbers increased rapidly to 15,500 by 1872 (Hastings and Turner 1965, 40). Several other factors encouraged the development of the southwestern cattle industry. Railroads were opened up across southern and northern Arizona in the early 1880s, which provided access to more grazing land, provided transportation to cattle markets, and brought more emigrants through and settlers into the region. More mineral discoveries in southern Arizona near the Southern Pacific railway spurred still more settlement activity. All of this was intensified by a public opinion that cattle ranching in Arizona was "easy money" (Osgood 1929, 86). Numerous cattle companies supplied meat to the newly founded and rapidly growing communities. By the mid-1880s nearly all available rangelands in Arizona were occupied (Haskett 1935, 35). Cattle numbers during this growth period are estimated at an astonishing 720,000 for southern Arizona and 1.5 million for all of Arizona in 1891 (Bahre and Shelton 1996, 9). A relatively stable Arizona cattle industry was established after nearly two hundred years. But just as soon as the industry became profitable, cattle production far outstripped local market needs. In response, and for the first time, Arizona cattle growers had to ship their product to markets outside the territory. Moreover, the stability of the 1880s gave way to crisis in the 1890s. Overgrazing of rangelands and cyclical drought severely degraded the once lush grasslands, and desertification tempered the industry's viability.

Cattle Hunting

We divide O'odham livestock history into two periods: cattle hunting, from 1697 to 1870, and cattle raising, from 1870 to the present. Cattle and horses, but also sheep, oxen, burros, goats, and chickens were initially imported into the region by the Jesuit missionary Eusebio Kino as incentives for Christian conversion and resettlement (Bolton 1919, 93; Fontana 1976, 60). The twenty-five missions Kino established were adjacent to perennial rivers, and each of them except San Xavier del Bac were a substantial distance from the Tohono O'odham. It is debatable whether or not the first domesticated animals supplied by Kino made much of an impact on the O'odham. Hackenberg (1983:166) argues that although livestock were accepted by the Tohono O'odham, they were unfamiliar with herding techniques and simply turned cattle loose on the range and hunted them when meat was desired. Cattle hunting was the first substantial way that the O'odham used cattle.

After Kino's death, missionary activities in O'odham territory were limited and sporadic. The Jesuit Order was expelled from the New World in 1767. The Franciscan Order replaced them, but the order had minimal contact with the O'odham except with those who continued residing in the former Jesuit mission communities. Apache raids on missions and other European outposts dampened their missionary efforts. The Franciscans did nonetheless continue with the delivery of livestock to the missions in their charge. For example, Kessell (1969, 57) notes that in 1821 the Tumacacori Mission had more than 5,000 head of cattle and 600 horses. This mission, on the southeastern periphery of O'odham territory, was a place where some Pima and O'odham lived and worked as ranch hands. Here the O'odham learned European ranching techniques, including horsemanship and roping, and this new knowledge eventually spread through the desert as people moved back and forth (Wagoner 1952, 12). It was likely here that the O'odham language was modified to reflect Spanish cattle culture at this mission and nearby *ranchos*. A review of O'odham descriptive nouns for cattle culture reveal Spanish-derived cognates. By examining a word list in O'odham, Spanish, and English, it is obvious that O'odham adopted Spanish rather than English usage (table 2.1). This suggests, following Herzog's (1941) language hypothesis, that the O'odham cattle-ranching vocabulary identifies the period when the O'odham incorporated these nouns, and therefore the objects themselves, into their language and practical use. The words, objects, and practices derive from the Spanish-speaking world, the earliest and most pronounced influence on O'odham cattle culture.

The Apaches continued to disrupt the region until the mid-1870s. Apache horsemen ran off the Spanish settlers and missionaries, and after 1821 kept the Mexicans from recolonizing the area. The O'odham considered the Apache to be enemies: the O'odham word for Apache *(o:b)* also means enemy. An example of Apache military effectiveness against the O'odham was recorded on a San Xavier calendar stick (a mnemonic device). During the summer of 1852, the village of Kui Tatk (Mesquite Root) was attacked and nearly all of its inhabitants

Table 2.1
O'odham, Spanish, and English Nouns related to Cattle Industry

O'odham	Spanish	English
*haiwañ	vaca	cow
kawiyu	caballo	horse
manayo	manada	untamed horse (mustang)
po:tol	potro	bronco
wu:lo	burro	donkey
wisilo	becerro	calf
ispul	espuela	spurs
si:l	silla	saddle
si:nju	cincho	cinch
istliw	estribo	stirrup
liat	lariat	lariat
capa li:ya	chaparreras	chaps
*wijina	cuerda	rope
wakial	vaquero	cowboy
*ṣawant or *hu'uida	rodeo	roundup
wi:lant	vela	vigil
la:nju	rancho	ranch

*Denotes words that have neither a Spanish nor an English cognate. Each of the four nouns was used in the context of deer hunting.

killed by Apaches (Underhill 1938a, 21–22). The Apache were so intimidating and effective that they forced the evacuation of the entire eastern portion of O'odham territory. Apache-O'odham warfare put a temporary halt to the O'odham's two-villager settlement pattern, forcing the O'odham to sequester themselves into ten defense villages.

Agricultural produce was the mainstay during the period of defense-village occupation because hunting made a hunter vulnerable to Apache raiders. The ability to rely on agricultural produce is surprising if the usual precariousness of O'odham agriculture is considered. What made this agriculture possible was a wetter than normal period while they were sequestered in the defensive villages. Schumm and Hadley (1957, 162) report that between approximately 1825 and 1875, tree and other vegetation growth and rainfall were at maximum, above-normal levels. We suggest that the above-normal moisture permitted the O'odham to cultivate wheat and other crops in sufficient amounts to feed themselves.

The Treaty of Guadalupe Hidalgo in 1848, the Gadsden Purchase of 1854, and the end of the Civil War signaled a turn in Apache-O'odham relations. The U.S. government gradually gained military control over the territory that the Spaniards and then Mexicans had ceded to the Apache. Apache raids were largely halted in the 1870s[5] by the U.S. military, whose numbers increased after the Civil War. Checking Apache resistance and incarcerating them on reservations had a dramatic effect on O'odham life. Most significantly, they moved away from the ten defense villages. This movement coincided, in the mid-1870s, with the resumption of drought conditions and resultant below-normal plant growth (see Schumm and Hadley 1957). It is unclear to what extent the renewed drought conditions spurred this relocation or dispersal away from the defense villages. With less than optimal precipitation, wheat and other crops could no longer be grown in quantities sufficient for continued sequestered settlement. In fact, the historical record is unclear whether drought, cessation of warfare with the Apache, or even population rebound after epidemics of infectious diseases (smallpox, influenza, etc.), or some combination of the above caused the dispersal. What is known is that the population dispersal led to a new form of O'odham residence patterns, the so-called Mother-Daughter village complexes. Villagers from nearly each of the ten defensive (Mother) villages moved away to found smaller satellite (Daughter) villages. These village complexes did maintain close economic, political, and ceremonial affiliations, and spouses were exchanged within them. The village complexes flourished over the next three decades. By 1920 R. Jones (1969) counted nearly 150 O'odham villages. The apex of dispersal, of founding new villages (approximately 1910), was reached simultaneously with the resumption of plentiful rainfall and plant growth. This indicates that, without a drought, it was no longer necessary for the population to continue its dispersal into unexploited resource areas. After 1920 yet another change occurred in village composition and residence patterns. Daughter village abandonments began, whereby residents returned to Mother villages or to other villages. This process of population concentration has continued to the present, and there are now approximately sixty occupied O'odham villages.

During the period of dispersal away from the ten defense villages and of developing Mother-Daughter village networks, cattle hunting gained importance in the O'odham subsistence practices of gathering, hunting, and floodwater agriculture and largely replaced the hunting of wild game. This substitute occurred because game populations dwindled as more Mexican and then U.S. settlers and miners moved into the area, overhunting game animals. The O'odham made no effort to corral the cattle that roamed their ranges. They were simply allowed to run wild, and they were considered much like deer or other game, to be hunted as needed (Xavier 1938, 2). Each family group had one or two appointed hunters, who ordinarily supplied ten or fifteen deer per year for the family. Family hunters obtained about the same number of semiwild cattle as they did deer, to be distributed for food, gifts, and barter (Underhill 1946).

Hunting semiwild cattle became institutionalized in and was based upon preexisting O'odham practice. For one thing, deer hunters were specialists who were called "head-bearers" *(mo'obḍam),* a name derived from the deer-head disguise that hunters wore during the hunt. Usually working in pairs, the *mo'obḍam* circled a deer, driving it toward an assistant. One of the hunters would then shoot the deer when it came to within his range. This type of hunt was known as a roundup *(hu'uida),* the same word that would eventually be used to describe cattle roundups.

For another thing, it was the family patriarch who assigned a deer hunter, just as he did later for a cattle hunter and still later for a cowboy. Finally, there are striking similarities between deer and cow songs. Bahr et al. (1979) suggest the existence of a thematic relation between deer and cow songs in that the lyrics of some songs suggest behavioral similarities.

O'odham Cattle Raising

In time, the hunting of semiwild cattle turned into the grazing and active management of small herds. This transition was due partly to the dispersals away from the ten defense villages. Many of the new Daughter villages were established near the wells dug by Mexican and

Anglo settlers in the southeast part of the reservation that had been abandoned because of Apache warfare. In 1914 the U.S. federal government began to drill wells and make range improvements that fostered the creation of some new villages and accompanying small herds. Couple the dispersal process away from defense villages with the influx of cattle from both Mexican and Anglo sources, and with the creation of cattle markets, and by the 1890s some O'odham had entered successfully into the regional cattle industry of Arizona (Spicer 1962, 138).

The O'odham's expanding livestock industry led to still other modifications in social life. Cattle raising and consumption eventually replaced agricultural and gathered produce as the O'odham increased their red-meat consumption. A diet of Mexican-influenced dishes such as red chile stew, dried beef, and tamales became the O'odham's "traditional" diet, a diet that is still considered "traditional." Reliance on agriculture had always been risky in this part of the desert and was perhaps easily replaced by cattle growing, a less risky food-getting strategy. Cattle also supplied money, something that their agriculture did not. By the turn of the century, the O'odham were differentially part of the regional cash economy. Importantly, the cowboy had also become a central aspect of O'odham male identity.

DL: It was my boy Wayne that really got interested in cowboying. He was a born cowboy. When he was real young, a toddler, every time that I saddled a horse, and would be riding it around, he wanted to ride with me. He would point, lift up his hand and point at me, and he'd be saying, "Uh-uh-uh-uh," to try to get his mom's attention, saying that he wanted to ride with me. So I'd go pick him up. His mom would lift him up to me, and I'd ride him around on horseback.

He started kindergarten over here in Santa Rosa, and every time he got off for lunch breaks he would run back to the house to play with his toys. He liked to play with his trucks and horses. He was really interested in horses. And I found out that he was a born cowboy. So I just let him do what he wanted to do with horses. I bought him a horse called Prince that was his own to ride around. He was very tame and gentle. He rode it around all of the time. And when Wayne started to grow up I let him ride in front of me, then let him ride behind me. Then I let him ride in front of me to train him how to use the bridle, how to turn it round, how to stop it, and how to do all this. Here he was really interested in horses.

At times when he'd be playing with other kids, and I'd be working in the horse pen, I might want him to water the horses. And as soon as I said "Wayne" and his mom would say that "he's not here, he's over there playing with the cousins," I'd ask her to "call him over because I want him to go water the horses." It was just a little ways, walking distance from the house. And then she'd call him, "Wayne, your dad wants you to water the horses." And as soon as she said something about the horses, he'd just come running. And I'd say, "Go water the horses." I'd put the bridle on Prince and put Wayne on the horse's back without the saddle. Then he'd walk the horse over there, water it, come back, and ride around for a while. This horse was real tame, and he would just slide off the horse when he wanted to play with the kids again. I found out that he wants to be a cowboy, so I just let him do these things.

But when he got sick in the first grade, well, he wasn't sick, but a doctor found out that his heart was bleeding. One of the vessels was blocked, the heart's blood was not running the way it was supposed to. So they said they were going to do open-heart surgery on him. And he was about five years old. So I kind of didn't like it because I didn't want to lose him. His doctor said that he had a fifty-fifty chance. The doctor said, "If you will let us do it, he will be a healthy young man. But if you don't let us do it, then you're going to lose him because his blood is not going to the part that it's supposed to be going to."

He was so skinny at that time, and we called him *s-gagui,* which means skinny in Papago. And his late uncle Andrew Aguila who stayed with us called him *pi gigcu,* which also means skinny. And after the surgery, after a time, he got better, and he was real happy to come back to us. So he got really well, and we left the hospital, came back home, but we were called over to the hospital again, and we went.

Anyway, like I said about Wayne, after we brought him home from the hospital, the doctor told us to not put him back to school until he told us that it would be all right. So he stayed away from school for six months. Boy, when we got him home he wanted to ride his horse. But the doctor said not to let him ride horses until he got better because he was not really healed yet. So he waited and waited until the doctor OK'd it, and another year went by. And here he wanted to ride his horse, and I keep telling him, "No, you're not gonna ride the horse until the doctor says that it is OK." So the doctor finally OK'd it, and boy, Wayne was just all smiles to be on his horse once again. He would just ride and ride, and I didn't say anything to him, because that was his own horse, and he wanted to be a born cowboy. So I just let him do whatever he wanted to do. And at that time, after about two years, and when he was OK, there was a junior rodeo at the school. So he wanted to ride a bull calf, and I OK'd it. I bought him western-style pants and shirt, and he already liked western clothes. I also bought him a hat, scarf, necktie, boots, spurs, chaps, and bull-riggin', and all that stuff. So that's his first rodeo when he was age seven. And then he got interested in riding bulls in other rodeos. And when he grew up, he started going to other places for rodeos, like in Sells, and to the Four Indian Nation Finals of Sacaton. And he was really interested in it. When he become old enough to handle his own horses, at the age of seven or so, he started going on roundup with us, going out rounduping with us.

At that time Baptisto was roundup boss, and we'd go up into the mountains. One time we were chasing the herd into a green meadow that is called Da'iwuñig. We were chasing the herd, and his grandpa, Baptisto Lopez, saw that Wayne was really chasing something. He thought he was chasing a cow. Baptisto went after him and discovered that he was chasing a wild pig. And Baptisto said to Wayne, "Leave that alone, that's a wild pig!" And he started laughing, and Wayne finally let go, and here he thought it was a cow or calf, he didn't know what it was. And they came up to the windmill where I was trapping cows when the other cowboys bring them in. Baptisto started telling the other cowboys what had happened, and the late Joe Listo started laughing. And his other grandpa Klasteen started laughing at him too: He said, "How come you chased it?" Wayne said, "I thought that it was a cow, I didn't know it was a pig. And then my grandpa came and said to 'let it go, it's a wild pig,' so I just let it go." So the other cowboys started laughing at him, and he become a real good cow hand. So he is a born cowboy.

Then later on when he grew up I taught him how to break horses, wild horses, *poptoliga,* we call them. And he started doing his own, and it's just the way that I had taught. My cousin, Regis Joaquin, is the same way. And he was another born cowboy. I taught him the same way to ride horses and work on roundups. My late cousin Amando Francisco, Regis, and I would go out horseback riding together to help stray cows in the desert, and to ride them [the horses]. And Regis, I'm the one who taught him, and now he is sick and can't ride horses, but he is still interested in them. Every time when we used to drink together and every time he sees me he always tells me that I'm the one: "You're the one who taught me all this, nobody else taught me how to cowboy. I remember that when I was a kid and you told me, 'Get on this horse, get on this horse, don't be afraid, get on it and ride it,' and I would do what you told me. And I'm glad that you did. I learned from you, and you're the only one who taught me how to ride and how to handle horses and how to do all of that cowboy job." And here he was a good cowboy. Regis also joined the rodeo at times to ride bulls.

And so those two are really interested in cowboying. And of my kids it was Wayne who is the only one who was really interested in roundups and horses. And he is now going out working with the other cowboys. And now that I'm not healthy, Wayne drives my truck around during roundup.

A few men in the southeast part of the Sells reservation became cattle owners with business in mind. In fact, the early move to commodity cattle production occurred in this part of O'odham territory. Further cattle introductions by Mexican and Anglo settlers from the 1870s onward served to stimulate O'odham cattle ranching practices. Spicer notes,

> some Papagos worked as cowboys and learned a great deal about cattle raising. On the west side of the Baboquivari Mountains some Papagos began the transition from subsistence cattle raising, involving a few

> cattle on unfenced range to be slaughtered when food was needed, to the planned raising of cattle for the national beef market. Beginning in the 1890s, family groups in this favorable area which included villages such as San Miguel, Chukut Kuk, Topawa, and Vamori began to improve water holes and to appropriate for their own use, in the manner of the White cattlemen, these water sources. Slowly they began to build up cattle herds which brought them into the cash economy of the region. (Spicer 1962, 138)

Several things contributed to this orientation in the southeastern part of the reservation: grasses were plentiful in this wetter section of the desert; the O'odham of the southern area had worked for wages as cowboys on Mexican *ranchos* and as laborers in their mines; and in the late 1890s, Protestant missionaries with their emphasis on the individual made inroads into this part of the reservation.[6]

Between 1900 and 1920, six informal grazing and roundup units were created. Of the six, one was distinctly larger than the others and has been classified by R. Jones (1969) as a "big roundup community." The big roundup community was comprised of the villages of Chukut Kuk, San Miguel, and Topawa on the western slope of the Baboquivari Mountains. The small roundup units were centered around the villages of Gu Achi, Sil Nakya, Stoa Pitk, Pisinimo, and Gu Oidak. It has been suggested that the so-called big roundup community represented a fundamental shift away from agriculture, community organization, and ceremonial observance (Xavier 1938; Spicer 1962; Underhill 1946). While very few individuals and families could support themselves with cattle sales alone, ranching did highlight a basic economic and social transformation.

The development of the big roundup community signifies a shift to an economic orientation previously unknown among the O'odham. Whereas the single-village and multivillage (Mother-Daughter) community organization—including the small roundup communities—was the norm at that time and identifiable by an agriculture orientation and ceremonial participation, the big roundup community was cattle (capitalist) oriented. What distinguishes membership in the single- and multivillage type is a local community allegiance with an emphasis on cooperation, sharing, folk-Catholicism, and native ceremonial life. The small roundup community continued to value those things that were culturally O'odham.

Diverging from this single- and multivillage pattern is the economic self-interest and the marketplace emphasis of the big roundup community. Life in the big roundup community ceased to be integrated by agriculture, sharing, extended family and community obligations, and the ceremonial life so important to people in the single- and multivillage community, who continued to depend on rain for their crops and spiritual well being. This is not to say that members of the big roundup community eschewed their O'odham identity. There is no evidence to make that claim. Rather, people of the big roundup community reordered their priorities, both economic and social.

Along with the frontier cattle economy came horses. Whereas cattle became commodities for sale, a store of food, and a personal bank account, horses became a cowboy's prize possession and companion. Horses became highly valued and esteemed animals for several reasons. They are often called pets *(ṣoṣoiga)* and are loved by their owners, who take great pride in them. A horse's value was and is not due to any economic value these animals may possess, which is low. Rather, a cowboy comes to rely on his horse; he is dependent upon it while on the job. Good horsemanship is highly prized among O'odham, and a good cowboy is worth a lot. Horses are also a source of prestige. Joseph et al. (1949, 59) note,

> Horses, rather than cattle, are the prestige animals. They are often of little economic value, at least in the numbers owned by the Papago, for many more are kept than can be used for farm and range work. . . . A Papago does not ordinarily know exactly how many head of cattle he has, *but he knows and is proud of every horse.* Cattle are merely his bank or source of food; they are a means to an end and not like horses, an end in themselves.
>
> Together, cattle and horses furnish food, money, transportation, prestige, and the excitement of the rodeo and roundup. To many a Papago a good field, enough cattle to provide occasional meat and money, a few horses for prestige, and plenty of rain would make an ideal combination.

DK: In addition to prestige and their utilitarian value, horses are also esteemed because they are a class of supernaturally powerful spirits. The horse's place in the O'odham imagination is most clearly illustrated by the fact that they entered into the O'odham's theory of sickness and cure, that a horse *(kawiyu)* can cause staying sickness, and that they are companions to devils. The cow *(haiwañ)* too has entered into this medical system, although to a lesser extent. Both animal species visit people's dreams, cause sickness, and give curative song poems. But horses appear to do so with more frequency. That horses and cattle have been incorporated into O'odham shamanism is no minor point. Their inclusion raises the fundamental question of why these animals entered the O'odham's imagination as spirit or power animals, as beasts of burden. Was it because the horse and cow are potentially dangerous animals due to their size and aggressiveness, because they represented wealth for Europeans, because they accompanied the arrival of the Spaniards, because the animals were physically different from other animal species in their experience? (After all, chickens and cats have not attained the status of cattle and horses.) It is all of these and one thing more.

Livestock presented the O'odham with two alien animal species and a new mode of production. While hunting, gathering, and agricultural forms of production all had mythico-religious grounding, the newly acquired cattle and horses did not. These animals had to be reconciled with their extant worldview. Cattle and horses were reconciled and found their place in the O'odham theory of sickness and cure. While it is not known and is unknowable exactly how these sicknesses evolved in the O'odham medical system, it is reasonable to suggest that the more people came into contact with these animals, the more injuries they suffered, and the more they attributed afflictions to them. As with most O'odham staying sicknesses, it is close contact and a human's knowing or unknowing mistreatment of the spirit entity that causes an illness. Once the unique properties of horses and cattle became understood by shamans—by being tutored by the spirits of these animals—and were understood to cause distinct kinds of illness and how they could be cured, these animals entered the O'odham theory of sickness and cure. This incorporation provided O'odham with the means to safely interact and cope with the supernatural aspect that these unusual animals presented. By medicalizing the relationship between humans and horses and cattle, the O'odham developed a way to heal

Table 2.2
Livestock Estimates and Counts, 1914–1974

Year	Horses	Cattle	Animal Units	Source
1914	8,000	30,000		Castetter and Bell (1942)
1914	2,000	14,000		Clotts (n.d.)*
1919	30,000	30,000		Metzler (1960)
1937		25,000		Xavier (1938)
1939	18,000	27,000		Metzler (1960)
1949			21,626	Kelly (1974)
1950	7,000	13,000		Metzler (1960)
1959			17,487	Kelly (1974)
1960		15,000		Woodbury and Woodbury (1962)
1962	4,770	10,082	16,070	Kelly (1974)
1966	4,458	16,146		U.S. Dept. of Commerce (1975)
1967	3,000	18,000		Simpson (1968)
1974	3,440	18,394		BIA (1974)

*Clotts estimated that these numbers could be as high as 8,000 to 10,000 horses and 30,000 to 50,000 cattle.

the sicknesses that, indirectly at least, the new mode of production generated.

By 1920 livestock numbers had grown considerably (table 2.2). This growth is seen by Woodbury and Woodbury (1962) as the result of the government well-drilling program initiated in 1913, in addition to wells sunk or enlarged by Mexican and Anglo ranchers illegally squatting on O'odham land. The wells assured a steady water supply in areas that previously had remained parched for most of the year and were largely incapable of supporting domestic animals. In 1914, according to Castetter and Bell (1942), there were between 30,000 and 50,000 head of cattle and approximately 10,000 horses on the reservation.

By 1919 livestock numbers peaked at around 30,000 head each of cattle and horses (Metzler 1960). By 1930, due to overgrazing and drought conditions, the federal government suggested limits on the numbers of stock animals a person or family could possess and strongly urged immediate stock reductions, herd development, and range improvements. In 1944 the Bureau of Indian Affairs (BIA) determined that the carrying capacity of the entire Sells reservation was 11,000 cattle and 1,000 horses (Bauer 1971, 88). The O'odham consistently resisted stock reductions, and tribal reduction initiatives went largely unenforced and unenforceable. Bauer (1971, 97) said,

> A primary reason for this intransigence [to grazing ordinances] is a result of the successful political opposition of a few cattle "baron" families [in the southeast grazing area]. These families are politically influential . . . because they employ or otherwise patronize the small Papago cattle owners and through this patronage (in effect) they control 90 percent of the range. . . . Ordinances would restrict their [the large cattle owners'] freedom.

Periodic drought conditions and a dourine (equine syphilis) epidemic substantially reduced O'odham herds by 1940. A stock reduction of horses was begun in 1934, when the state of Arizona destroyed thousands of dourine-infected animals. Severe drought also caused many smaller livestock owners to loose all of their animals.

In 1935 the BIA divided the O'odham (Sells) reservation into nine grazing districts (two additional districts were made of the San Xavier and Gila Bend reservations). District boundaries were loosely established along precattle, hunting and gathering use-areas. It was also in 1935 that the BIA established a collective tribal herd and created the Livestock Board and livestock associations that were composed and run primarily by the O'odham "cattle barons." During the 1950s many of the districts implemented their own livestock associations.

By 1960 the yearly total of gross receipts of cattle sales reached three-quarters of a million dollars (Manuel et al. 1978, 532), with approximately 10,000 head sold annually (BIA, Papago Agency 1974). Although it seems high, this figure is misleading. Metzler (1960, chapter 4, 6) notes that in 1959 less than 5 percent of the O'odham owned about 80 percent of the livestock. Bauer (1971, 89) mentions that by 1970 there were only a dozen or so families that raised cattle as an industry. Kelly (1974, 78) notes that the BIA estimated that seven families owned between 200 and 600 head of cattle each and that ten families possessed about 100 to 150 head, while most families had 10 head or less or none at all. These small holders are estimated at between 400 and 500 families. These numbers suggest that from when O'odham first began herding cattle up to 1970, a concentration of wealth accompanied this developing industry, and only a handful of families possessed more than a few head of cattle for subsistence. These estimates supply evidence of a class-based division between large and small holders.[7] While we could not secure more recent accountings, anecdotal evidence from our discussions with contemporary cowboys confirms that this division still existed in the 1980s and 1990s. Many O'odham said that, if anything, the concentration has become even more pronounced today than twenty-five years ago.

O'odham cattle raisers and ranchers use two distinct marketing strategies, which depend on the number of cattle owned. Large cattle ranchers market their holdings to realize a profit, while most O'odham sell only in times of need. Profit-seeking cattlemen hold a limited number of auctions and sales per year, where they sell in bulk, usually at market prices. In contrast to this calculated marketing strategy, the majority of small-holding, subsistence cattle raisers sell their livestock in small numbers, perhaps only one at a time, for far below market prices. These O'odham have cultivated a relationship with a cattle buyer from Tucson, Casa Grande, or Phoenix who comes to the reservation and buys one or a few head at a time for far less than market value. The relations between buyer and O'odham can be likened to a patron-client relationship, where the buyer is a person whom an O'odham can turn to in times of economic crisis (Fontana 1976, 64).

Cattle, Class, and Conflict

The preceding discussion illustrates the background and formation of a dual class structure among the O'odham. This dual class structure had the side effect of generated class-based tensions, animosities, and envies. It is a case where material and ideational changes occurred in the context of culture change.

Prior to 1890 the big roundup community and large livestock owners did not exist. Livestock, a cash economy, and Protestant missionization are the material objects and ideational influence that pushed O'odham from a society where age, gender, and supernatural alliances defined status to one where wealth accumulation became equated with status and political power. On the one hand, members of the small roundup communities, although actively raising cattle, did so largely as a supplement and modest contribution to their mixed subsistence activities. And even if selling cattle was part of this mixed economy, cash sales comprised only a small portion of it. Profiting from their cattle holdings was not an end the small holder strove for.

On the other hand, there was a growing emphasis on cattle entrepreneurism, on profit, and on individual self-interest and the resultant waning of both folk Catholic and aboriginal ceremonialism in the big roundup community. Money for those in this community became an end goal. Cattle became a money-making industry. Commodity cattle ranching in the big roundup community encouraged a different variety of O'odham culture than that found in the single- and multivillage community (Jones 1969, 497). We believe that the cultural difference is based in the formation of a two-class society. The fact that most O'odham were eventually drawn into this economic transformation, and that a minority of O'odham were more financially successful than others, points to social differentiation based in economic relations, and therefore away from the conventional O'odham basis of social differentiation of age, gender, and interpersonal intercourse.

The ethnographic and historical record are sprinkled with anecdotal evidence suggesting that from the very beginning of O'odham cattle ranching, there was a conceptual, in addition to an economic, division established between large and small cattle holders. Early in the twentieth century, for instance, roundups were initiated by large cattle owners since they had the most vested interest in cattle and in assuring that their interests were well served. Underhill (1939, 208) found that among cattle ranchers in the south, approximately six extended families herded their cattle together and were led by a patriarch. Of these ranches Underhill (1939, 208) said, "There are six establishments . . . which merit the term of cattle ranches and their patriarchal heads are powerful persons, whose neighbors give them a feudal obedience." Xavier (1938) also documented the role that these patriarchs played in community life, leading lives of prestige and social and political influence.

The owners of large herds transformed their economic resources into personal political power. Economically based power subverted the traditional political process of status and political power as the result of good deeds, wisdom, and old age. Prestige based on economics rivaled and challenged that of prestige based upon community service, ceremonial leadership, and political office. In the big roundup community, the latter was usurped by the former.

Conflicts arose when wealth disparities made the small holder question how wealthy cattlemen obtained their wealth and what they spent it on. Often, the answer was and still is that they had made an agreement with devils or that they used sorcery. Underhill (1939, 209–10) observed as much when she said, "The majority . . . tend to regard them [rich cattlemen] with resignation, as people successful by supernatural means. If kinsmen, they expect gifts from them: if strangers, they tend to accuse them of mysterious luck much in the nature of sorcery." This fundamental suspicion has consequences for the wealthy. For instance,

> some men, misers, have hundreds of cattle. They are criticized for receiving more help than they give at roundups. . . . The cattle misers have stayed aloof from the present institutions [Catholic feasting, ceremonial sponsorship]. . . . They are said to be buried with lard cans full of their unspent silver dollars. We can regard them as outside the generosity system. . . . Lard buckets of silver dollars are proofs that their deceased owner didn't get anywhere in Papago society. (Bahr 1964:5)

It should be understood that people are criticized not so much because they have money but for how they use it, or, as in the above quote, refuse to use it. Does a person use money modestly and in the interest of others? Does the rich cattle rancher give gifts to kinsmen, sponsor village feasts and other church activities? Or does he spend it openly, publicly, cynically, for his self-gratification? Does the rich O'odham purchase new vehicles or saddles and always wear new clothes? How these questions are answered partly determines how others view that person's integrity. For O'odham, money is neither good nor bad in any intrinsic sense. Rather, a person is viewed as good or bad depending on how they use their money.

DK: The devil has begun to occupy the anthropological imagination and is most often described as a symbol of social disruption, of unequal economic relations, gender disputes, and the perils of the capitalist mode of production. Theoretically the devil provides a fertile area for considering native responses to the effects of global capitalism. Furthermore, the devil certainly provides a unique window into the dynamics of culture change. Devil beliefs such as those of the O'odham are not unique. In fact, devil beliefs and devil-lore are a widespread phenomenon in the native New World. The ethnographic reportage on devil beliefs in the Americas is perhaps becoming a subgenre of anthropological writing, much like the millennial cargo cult subgenre in the native Pacific region. A partial list of devil studies includes cases from the following countries: Bolivia (Harris 1982, 1989; Nash 1972, 1979; Taussig 1980, 1987), Brazil (Gross 1983), Colombia (Taussig 1980), Ecuador (Crain 1991, 1994), Mexico (Behar 1987; Cervantes 1994; Crumrine 1977; Friedlander 1990; Ingham 1986; Kennedy 1978; Merrill 1988), Nicaragua (Edelman 1994), Peru (Parry 1989; Silverblatt 1980, 1987), Trinidad (Alonso 1990), and the United States (Painter 1988). Although only a few of the above culture studies take the devil as their primary subject, they all describe devil beliefs and practices, and several argue that the devil is a multivocalic symbol expressive of complex cultural historic events and processes. Devils are said to variously signal the tumultuous process of Christian missionization, political subjugation, economic incorporation and transformation, capitalization, and gender and ethnic tensions. Some scholars also find that devils express a local discontent within the bounds of the community, and devil beliefs are often if not always linked to envy, jealousy, and sorcery.

Michael Taussig's *The Devil and Commodity Fetishism in South America* (1980) is perhaps the most widely read and influential anthropological work on native devil beliefs. I will not review his entire argument here but will outline a few significant points relative to the present work. Taussig's theory-driven analysis of Bolivian tin miners and Colombian Cauca Valley sugar cane cutters posits a relation between these peoples' supposedly recent proletarianization and their devil beliefs. He claims that devil beliefs are grounded in and derive directly from capitalist economic exploitation and that indigenous people recognize an implicit linkage between them. Taussig constructs a theoretical and highly idealized dichotomy, arguing that these peasants recognize through their devil beliefs that a fundamental distinction exists between an indigenous and moral agrarian (use-value) peasant economy, and an immoral capitalist (exchange-value) mode of production and economic system. He argues that peasant and traditional agricultural labor and production are viewed by peasants as fertile and moral, while proletarian labor and production are seen as infertile and immoral. Money earned from wage labor in mines, for instance, is conceived of as sterile because of its relation to the devil, and it can therefore only be used to purchase luxury goods (liquor, cigarettes, prostitutes), while money obtained from the sale of one's harvest of the land is fertile and can be safely reinvested in one's land and home. It is proposed that agriculture reproduces community because it is fertile, whereas capitalist labor undermines community because it is sterile and inherently divisive.

This theoretical construct does not fit O'odham devil way. While money is viewed by some as dangerous and disruptive, this attitude is largely the product of how humans choose to use it. Money, whether earned through the sale of cattle or by working in mines or in the homes of whites in Tucson as domestics, can be either good or bad. There simply is no sense of some intrinsic evil unique to money and capitalism.

The theoretical roots of Taussig's dichotomy originate in Marx's compelling ideas on use-value and exchange-value economics, and in commodity fetishism. Taussig's dichotomizing is not new to anthropology (Appadurai 1986, 11), and it continues to be a popular interpretive and analytic device. Taussig invokes this construct to classify and explain why peasants view capitalism with contempt and loathing, and why they resist it. According to him, peasant devil beliefs symbolize and rationalize the dangers and dehumanization of the capitalist mode of production. His conclusion is that tin miner and plantation laborer devil beliefs are an indigenous form of social protest and resistance, a native critique of money as evil, and a rejection of the alienating and debilitating effects of the capitalist mode of production. A provocative analysis, but is it historically and ethnographically accurate?

Taussig has been criticized for minimizing the role of Christian history (Chevalier 1987) and the history of the Bolivian peasants' folk Catholicism (Harris 1989). He has also been criticized for claiming that devil pacts arose in Europe during a similar agrarian-capitalist transformation, when in fact such "pacts" trace to the sixteenth century, prior to capitalism (Gross 1983; McEachern and Mayer 1986; Russell 1984, 1986). He is said to have misread the convoluted labor history of the Bolivian tin miners' and Colombian cane cutters' proletarianization (Godoy 1985; Gross 1983; Roseberry 1989). Taussig assumes incorrectly that these Bolivian tin miners and Cauca Valley sugar cane cutters only recently entered the proletarian ranks and that devil pacts symbolize the peasant's being wrenched away from their precapitalist mode of production. It would appear that Taussig's interpretation has serious flaws, especially if one considers Nash's (1978) source ethnography.

Taussig has been criticized for essentializing the precapitalist:capitalist, moral:immoral dichotomy as a cultural fact (Roseberry 1989) and romanticizing the "pristine," precapitalist peasant life (Marcus 1986). His dichotomizing is perhaps ironic given that he bases an important segment of his interpretation on the research of Nash (1972, 1979), who found, contrary to Taussig's reading, a lengthy proletarian history among Bolivian tin miners (peasants). In fact, according to Nash, these miners were not only *not* mystified by capitalism, as Taussig claims, but they were one of the most highly organized labor-union and class-conscious groups in all of South America. Taussig's reason for rejecting Nash's original interpretation is that she employs a functionalist explanation, a theoretical framework that he says contributes to the peasant's continued exploitation and political oppression (Gross 1983, 701).

Despite these severe shortcomings, Mary Crain (1991) has replicated, with minor variation, Taussig's fundamental dualistic and theoretically deterministic model in an analysis of devil beliefs among Ecuadorian Quimsa peasants. Crain posits that devil possession is a coded language of resistance to capitalist penetration, as well as an ethnic boundary marker between peasants and dominant others. She places gender relations, male versus female, at the core of the moral peasant versus the immoral capitalist dualism, in which men do immoral capitalized labor while women work as moral precapitalists. Men are said to enter into devil pacts to increase their wage earnings while women continue their modest subsistence activities. Crain argues that women tell stories of devil possession, of the immoral behavior of men who embrace dubious capitalist values. Thus, she combines gender roles, economics, and politics to critique the contentious problems generated by capitalism while maintaining a dualist framework to present her data.

Unfortunately, Crain's analysis suffers many of the same problems as Taussig's. As Hirschkind (1994, 202) has pointed out, Crain's findings of a resistance to capitalism among Quimseño peasants probably derives from Crain herself rather than from the peasants she studies. Although Crain offers evidence of envy as a reasonable explanation, pointing out that women also produce commodities for sale in the marketplace and that men also engage in devil talk, she fails to consider this evidence seriously and settles for the preformulated answer that Quimseño devil beliefs are a form of capitalist resistance. Thus, both Taussig (1980) and Crain (1991) appear to masquerade their own political and social agendas as the "native point of view" they claim that they are re-presenting. In both, the facts do not add up to the interpretations and conclusions that they each draw. In both, the interpretations do not fit the ethnographic facts.

I am not philosophically averse to the desire to critique the exploitive realities of the capitalist mode of production, nor to the demonstration of how it is an alienating economic system. On the contrary, I believe that such theorizing and providing ethnographic examples have an important place in thinking about the New World devil phenomenon. However, this theorizing and analysis must be grounded in empirical observation and be data driven rather than theory driven.

Marc Edelman's (1994, 78) study provides an important corrective to both Taussig's and Crain's analyses by questioning the idea that devil-pact stories are a historically specific peasant reaction to a wage-labor-based agrarian capitalism, and Edelman questions whether or not devil beliefs represent an unambiguous critique of one particular variety of production relations. This is

> not to say that he considers capitalism an unimportant component of or influence on the devil phenomenon. His examination of devil pacts on cattle haciendas along the Nicaraguan Pacific coastal plains reveals that such beliefs are never unambiguous because they tend to merge economic (capitalist) exploitation with cultural and sexual domination, gender antagonisms, and unmet needs and desires. Edelman observes that devil pacts serve to simultaneously generate envy of and identification with those peasant men believed to have made prosperous devil pacts. He demonstrates the contradictory nature of devil beliefs in that devils stand for more than capitalist resistance, though it too is part of the equation.
>
> The ambiguity and symbolic complexity inherent in devil beliefs must lead to theorizing that is ethnographically informed. Devil theorizing provides a beginning but is not sufficient to analyze O'odham devil way. The O'odham devil phenomenon shares with previous analyses and ethnographic examples an element of devils as symbols of the immorality of capitalist relations, production, and the creation of envy. The O'odham devil phenomenon, however, is not an unambiguous critique of capitalism. As will be seen in the following chapters, to understand devil way one must entertain other nonmaterialist theoretical orientations. It is my contention, therefore, that O'odham devil beliefs and practices need to be analyzed from a multiplicity of theoretical perspectives because the ethnographic record is far too diverse to subsume it under one or another essentializing theory of resistance.

Current O'odham cattle activities are the result of a three-centuries-long process. From a subsistence-oriented economy, livestock served as a catalyst of tremendous social, economic, and political transformation. O'odham reliance on cattle—first hunted, then herded, and finally commoditized—increased parallel to the development of the Anglo Arizona cattle industry. Whereas the majority of O'odham continue to view cattle as a mode of subsistence, a minority of O'odham ranchers are cattle entrepreneurs. Subsistence and commoditized economic strategies exist side by side where they mingle during seasonal roundups, at livestock meetings, and at rodeos. Our reading of the historical and ethnographic record reveals that the O'odham cattle industry was the first significant source of economic stratification in O'odham society. Led by a few cattlemen, this development initiated, for the first time in O'odham history, an economic basis for status acquisition and political power, but also for significant wealth disparities. This economic transformation in O'odham culture from an egalitarian and community-based society to one divided by class has deeply altered the political and social framework of O'odham lives. But this transformation has also been related to cattle and horses and cowboy culture in general through their shamanic theory of sickness and cure, in which it is the wealthy cattleman, the *rancheros,* the cattle barons, that symbolize devils and acquisitive self-interest.

3

O'odham Cosmology and Devil Way

The culture history of O'odham devil way is a fusion of indigenous and Christian religious ideas and practices that were strongly influenced by the development of the regional Southwest cattle-ranching industry. Given the word devil *(jiawul),* a cognate of the Spanish *diablo,* it might at first seem that a *jiawul* is little more than an O'odham version of the Christian Satan image, with horns, tail, and scarlet flesh. This superficial image is inaccurate, however, because O'odham devils are derived more from indigenous O'odham cosmology than from Christian theology.

O'odham devils are spirits who appear as phantasms in the dreams of living humans. Devil phantasms are frequently described by the O'odham as themselves. That is, devils are deceased O'odham who take up residence in devil mountains upon death and who then participate in devil, cattle-ranching activities. Previous ethnographies report that devils may take human form (Bahr 1988a), appear horselike (Russell 1908), or sometimes appear in the Christian image of the devil (Underhill 1946). Devils have been correctly linked to the physical vicinity of ranches and mines and thus to the presence of European economic activity (Bahr 1988a). While these publications are correct, they provide only a partial description of the O'odham devil way.

The O'odham's Christianization coincided with their active engagement with cattle raising in the last quarter of the nineteenth century. Whereas the saint religion *(sa:nto himdag)* reflects the O'odham's acceptance of Catholicism around the turn of the century, devil way *(jiawul himdag)* reflects how the cattle industry, shamanism, and Christianity were fused in the O'odham historical imagination. This fusion

Da:m ka:cim
(up-above-laying)

Huduñig
(sunset)

Ka:cim jeweḍ
(staying earth)

Si'alig weco
(beyond-the-eastern-horizon)

Mehi weco
(fire below)

Figure 3.1
Tohono O'odham Cosmological Landscape

provides insight into how they interpreted and perceived not only the new economy and religion, but also themselves.

O'odham Cosmology and Way: *O'odham Himdag*

O'odham cosmology is based on an intersection between multiple vertical layers and a horizontal plane (fig. 3.1). The vertical layers are, from bottom to top, the fire below *(mehi weco),* the staying earth *(jeweḍ ka:cim),* and up-above-laying *(da:m ka:cim).* The vertical axis of hell, the earth, and heaven was strongly influenced by Christianity. The horizontal axis, which bisects the vertical, is native and includes the very important beyond-the-eastern-horizon *(si'alig weco),* the afterlife location of, at least ideally, all deceased O'odham. O'odham consider it much as Christians consider heaven, except that it has a distinctly O'odham appearance (more on this below). Moving westward is the horizontal plane's intersection with the vertical at the staying earth. The staying earth is where all humans, animals, and the natural world exist. Farther west on this journey, which by the way replicates the path of the sun and moon, is the sunset place *(huḍuñig).* Here is the ocean (Gulf of California), an important pilgrimage site for prospective shamans as well as a salt-gathering location. Some spirits are thought to dwell in the sunset place. Scattered over the horizontal plane are sacred mountains, caves, and shrines, where spirits and humans may interact.

O'odham cosmology is a world of souls or spirits. While there is no directly translatable word in O'odham for *soul* or *spirit, i:bdag* comes

Heaven
Residence of God, Christ, saints, Mary, devout non-O'odham Christians.

Sunset
Land of spirit animals, the ocean, and some devils.

Earth
Residence of humans and the natural world, including the mountain homes of devils and devil-owls.

Sunrise Below
Residence of all deceased O'odham. It is considered the flowery world.

Hell
Home to the Christian's Satan, fallen angels, and evil non-Indian humans.

Figure 3.2
The Human and Spirit-Filled World

close. *I:bdag* refers to the heart, and this is further linked to the word for breath *(i:bui),* because breath is animated by the heart.

Nearly all O'odham dead proceed to *si'alig weco.* This idyllic afterlife location, with plentiful rainfall, a green and lush landscape, beautiful fields of crops, and much wildlife, is where all of one's relatives and friends can be found, and where social dances and frivolity are on the main menu. The souls of all non-Indians go to either heaven or hell, and God or Christ *(Jioṣ)* and the saints *(sasantos)* inhabit an idyllic heaven (fig. 3.2).

The spirit of a deceased person can return from *si'alig weco* to visit their living ancestors in the form of an owl *(cukuḍ),* often because the spirit misses its living relatives. Such owl visitations are also a way for spirits to teach humans in the shamanic and curative arts. But deceased humans can also become spirits called devils (*jejawul*). An O'odham devil was a cowboy in life. Upon death the devil establishes residence in one or another of the devil mountains that dot the desert. Here the afterlife location is also idyllic in that the devil continues to do what he did in life—the cowboy job of riding horses, rounding up cattle, and so on. A third, and tragic, type of human spirit is the devil-owl *(jiawul-cukuḍ).* This person was a cowboy in life but one who died tragically and suddenly, in some violent manner. Perhaps most common of these spirits are those who died in automobile accidents. Roadside crosses mark the place of death (Kozak and Lopez 1991; Kozak 1994). Devil-owl spirits are troubling for the living because they are thought to remain at the location of their death. The spirits haunt and pester the living and endanger them because of the loneliness of their predicament.

Number-color-direction symbolism is undertheorized in the O'odham cosmology, at least when compared to the very elaborate Pueblo and Navajo cosmologies (Lamphere 1983, 762). One symbolic correlation is between direction and the color of clouds and the wind house *(hewel ki:)* that sits there. Colors are somewhat important in song-poetics because they assist in description and establishing mood in the song. The number four, and multiples thereof, is important in both song and native ceremonials. O'odham culture emphasizes dream journeys and power acquisition rather than priestly systems of the kind found in the kiva societies of the various Pueblos.

O'odham *himdag* (the people's tradition) comprises native beliefs and practices associated with the communal rites of world renewal *(wi:gita),*[1] rain dance *(gohimeli),* and sit- and-drink *(dahiwa k i:)*[2] as well as individual rites of power acquisition, including salt pilgrimages, eagle killing, warfare exploits (scalping enemies), the shamanic arts of diagnosis and cure, and sorcery. Dreaming played and continues to play an integral if not central part in both the communal and individual activities. And as Underhill (1946, 17–18) has noted, it appears that even individual power acquisition through dreaming has a communal benefit.

These aboriginal practices have gradually shrunk in importance over the course of the twentieth century, and many could be said to be moribund. While it is true that the *wi:gita* is still performed in Quitovac, Mexico (and is directed by U.S. O'odham from Menager's Dam or Ali Chuk), it is equally true that only a small proportion of all O'odham participate in or observe this ritual (see Galinier 1991). The same can be said of the *gohimeli* and sit-and-drink, although the *gohimeli* attracts more participants than the *wi:gita.* Because of reservation building, mandatory public education, Catholic and Protestant missions, water-well drilling, the seven-day week, wage labor, and television, these communal rituals have seemingly lost ground in their applicability in peoples' everyday lives: the O'odham no longer depend on the cycles of nature, cycles central to aboriginal agriculture.

To our knowledge, none of the individual rites of power getting, except for dreaming, are routinely experienced today.[3] Some people continue to dream new songs, and this remains an important part of O'odham experience and self identification. It is unknown, however, just how extensive song dreaming is. Is dreaming limited to a few shaman *(ma:kai)* and ritual curers *(s-wusos o'odham),* or is the dreaming of new songs still a widespread activity? We cannot answer this question. It is clear that the O'odham theory of sickness and cure with its medical practitioners comprise what most O'odham of today consider to be *o'odham himdag.*

We divide the O'odham theory of sickness and cure into three broad categories: staying sickness, wandering sickness, and sorcery. Each has identifying characteristics as well as shared attributes. Blanketing the O'odham homeland is a class of sicknesses unique to the O'odham, staying sickness *(ka:cim mumkidag),* which originated in the time of mythical creation. Staying sicknesses, according to O'odham myth, have a supernatural etiology. When asked about the origins of staying sickness, the late shaman Juan Gregorio had this to say:

> It [*ka:cim* sickness] never wanders,
> it only goes around here,
> because it is established here,
> [by] whatever thing [a god] gave it [commanded the order of all things, including sicknesses] to us,
> whatever made us and whatever he gave to us.
> And even though it [the commanded order] seems wrong,
> still it has its source in propriety
> which is the origin of that kind of sickness
> however many things he gave to us.
> It [*ka:cim* sickness] originates from that [given order] and it is only here,
> it [*ka:cim* sickness] only exists right here,
> and truly it only goes around here,
> it only applies to us. (Bahr et al. 1974, 38–39)

There are approximately forty known staying sicknesses that "have been here from the beginning," which are traceable to Earth Doctor *(Jeweḍ Ma:kai)* and Elder Brother *(I'itoi),* the man-god creator. They constitute a zoologically based theory of sickness whereby the spirits of animals (deer, badger, rabbit, gila monster, lizard, turtle, coyote, cow, bear, gopher) inflict their way *(himdag)* on humans. The spirit ways of deceased humans (ghost, whore, devil, saint, Apache), plants (jimson weed, peyote), natural phenomena (water, wind, lightning), birds (eagle, hawk, swallow, buzzard), and insects (fly, butterfly, bee) also cause types of staying sickness. A person may contract one or more of these sicknesses throughout a lifetime by intentionally or unintentionally violating the integrity *(cihañig)* of the way of one of these animals, humans, natural phenomena, birds, plants, or insects. Contracting sickness means that a human somehow showed disrespect for or mistreated—in other words, demeaned, physically harmed, or degraded—the type or class of spirit being. Each of these ways is considered to be a dangerous thing *(s-ta-e:bidam ha'icu)* because it has the ability to punish the human who mistreated it. And while sickness-causing spirits cause sickness, they also possess the knowledge of their distinct cure, and they give this knowledge to select humans during dreams. During a conversation, Lopez explained this phenomenon to Kozak in the following manner:

DK:

K hascu wuḍ hegam ha'icu	What are those
duakam o hehemajkam,	animals or people,
o abṣ cum hascu mo'am	just whatever
cecegid,	arrives
k'am ha'icu maṣcam	to teach things to
g hemajkam?	a person?

DL:

Mañ abṣ wo cei mo k	I'll just say what
hega'i map hab kaij,	you said,
mo abṣ hi'a cum hascu matp	that it's just whatever
hascu wo i wui jiwa g hemajkam	comes toward a person,
mo g jiawul, o g ko'o'i,	like the devil, rattlesnake,
o g komkicud, o g cukuḍ,	or turtle, or spirit-ghost,
o g mat p hascu wo i wui jiwa	or whatever will come toward
g hemajkam mat heg wo	the people that will
maṣca g hemajkam mat	teach the people
heg ab wo s-ma:c,	to be good at that,
k t g ñe'i, o g mumkidag.	the song, or the sickness.

C hekaj aba i abṣ	That's why it is just up to
g hemajkam,	the person,
mat p hascu woi ñe'id	whatever they will see
am e-kosc-uḍ,	in their sleep,
o abṣ cum has masma mat heg	or whatever way that
wo wui jiwa g hemajkam,	it will come to a human,
mat heg ab s-ma:c	that they'll be good at that
g mat heg e-wo maṣc,	and will learn,
g hemajkam t heg ab wo s-ma:c,	the people will learn that,
k heg wo hekaj g hega'i,	and will use that,
c eda ha'ic ama ha'icu,	and with others,
k ab e:p s-ma:c,	who will also learn well,
s-mai ha'icu wo s-ma:c,	or discover that they're good at [it],
k am i himdam am ha'icu,	and later on,
ep wo ñe'id ha'icu e:p,	they might see something else,
o s-ma:c g ba'ij'i, ge'e,	and will know that too, will learn much more,
ha'icu wo s-ma:c k mu'i ha'icu,	will learn many more things,
k s-mai ami dam.	and more on top of that.

DK:

T hascu a:g hega'i ha'icu	What does it mean that an
mat am ma:cul g hemajkam?	animal will teach a person?

DL:

Na'as hab a:g abṣ	It is just what it
an ma:culig hemajkam hega'i,	teaches the people,
map t has cei ha'icu i	that whatever
mat am ma:culig g hemajkam,	it teaches the person,
mat heg wo hekaj k heg ab	that person will use it and
wo s-ma:c k.	will be good at that.
Ha'ab abṣ am wo i himad,	So it just keeps continuing,
g mumkidag,	the sickness,
mat hab ab wo hekajkad	it keeps on going,
mo hemu hab e-wua,	like right now it happens,
c ha'icu pi e-ma:c	and sometimes they
pi e-mamc g mumkidag	don't understand the sickness,
mat ab hema k hab	but they will find out from
wo ñe'id ha'icu mumkidag.	someone who will see the sickness.

Heg hekaj hab e-wua	That's why they will
mat hema ha'icu ab wo ma:culid,	train some of them,
g hemajkam ba'ij'i	some of the people, so they
e:p wo s-ma:ckad e:p.	will know more about it.

DK:

K hascu wuḍ na:nko hegam	What is different about those
mamakai c s-wusos o'odham?	shamans and ritual curers?

DL:

Ma:kai, c hegam mo ha-wusot,	Shaman, and those who cure—
mo pi wuḍ mamakai,	those who are not shaman,
mo haba masma u'ukc	but those that get their
e-gewkdag mo g ma:kai,	strength just like the shaman,
(ma:kai mat wo ha-kulañmad),	(shaman who medicate)—
ba'ep wo ha-wuso wo ha-duaj,	they will also cure and sing,
k hegam mo pi wuḍ mamakai	and those that aren't shamans,
hia pi wo ha-kulañmad,	who will not doctor someone,
ṣ hab abṣ wo ha-wuso,	but will just cure them,
wo ha-wustan,	will blow on them,
k ñe'e ha'icu e:p—	and will sing for something—
ṣ heg wepo mo we:s	but it seems like it is
atp ama hegam,	all the same,
ha'icu i wepo hegam	the things that
ha'icu ama s-ñeid,	are seen,
heba'icu:c heba'i mamakai	and at times they will appear
wui o ha'icu jiwa.	in front of the shaman.
Masma mo g cukuḍ,	Things like the owl
o g jiawul wo wui	or a devil will approach
jiwa wo ha'icu ma:cul,	him and will train him,
c masma heba'i	and from this
ha'ic e-mamakaicuḍ	some become shamans
o s-wusos o'odham.	or ritual curers.
Mat hemu wo i e-ma:kaic mat wo	They just become new doctors when
ha'icu wui jiwa wo ha'icu	something appears and
maṣca,	trains him,
tk amjed wo e-ma:kaic.	and from that he will become a shaman.
Mat hemu amai ma:kai	Like right now there are
hegam mo ha-wusot,	those shamans who cure,

mat wo ha'icu wui
jiwa wo ha-a:g g ñeñe'i,
jiawul wo wui
jiwa k a:g g ñeñe'i,
o g cukuḍ wo wui
jiwa wo a:g
mat hascu ñeñe'i-kaj wo
ha-wuso
g hemajkam wo ha-duaj.
Ba masma hekaj atp
abṣ am i wes e-wepo masma.
Hab cu'ig ma:kai,
c hegam mo ha-wusot.
Ha-wui jejeawep,
hegam ha'icu hekaj s-mamce
ma:kai hab ab haba
e:p ha-wusot.
G ma:kai e:p ha-duajid
c e:p ha-kulañmad.
C idam mo ha-wusot
mo abṣ ha-wusot.
Mat abṣ s-cuhugamac wo ñe'i,
o heba 'i taṣeḍ
he'ekai ola ab wo ñe'i.
Ṣ hab-a ama wes e-wepo
hegam eda e-gewkdag,
hegam mo ha-wuso
ha'icu in ce'ecem
ha'icu in has juñim.

and something appears to them
and will tell them the songs,
a devil will appear
and will sing songs,
or a ghost-spirit will come
forward and tell
him what kinds of songs to use
to cure
the person in a diagnosis.
Then it is all the same
way, all the same.
It is like the shaman,
and those who just cure people.
Something will appear to them,
and that is why they know
things the shaman knows,
who can also cure them.
The shaman diagnoses them
and also medicates them.
And those who just blow,
they just cure people.
They will be singing at night,
or during the daytime,
any hour they will be singing.
However, both have the
same level of power,
those who cure
and those who diagnose.

DK: Key to a discussion of O'odham cosmology and theory of sickness and cure are several interrelated concepts. First, the difference between shamans and ritual curers is significant with regard to their medical roles. As is the case around the world, where cultures have a shamanic tradition, it is the shaman who is thought to be the more important practitioner because the correct diagnosis is imperative for an effective cure. The O'odham shaman has the ability to see *(ñeid)* into the bodies of the sick, whereas ritual curers do not. Seeing ability refers to the power of a shaman to contact his spirit tutularies, an ability not possessed by ritual curers. While spirits approach *(wui jiwa)* in order to teach *(maṣcam)* both shaman and ritual curers, it is the shaman who has the power *(gewkdag)* to invoke them for a diagnosis. To "blow" *(wuso)* is of critical importance to the shaman or the curer. Power, breath (to blow), and the heart are closely allied concepts. A shaman's diagnostic and curing abilities reside near the heart, where the spirit tutors aim their guidance.

Some ritual curers and shamans become identified as possessing one or another type of heart *(i:bdag)* related to a spirit type who has been a particularly important mentor for the person. The acts of singing and blowing are sacramental gestures.

Both shaman and ritual curers use things or techniques to enhance their abilities. In diagnostic sessions a shaman's breath can be enhanced with medicine tools or fetishes *(iagta)*. For instance, the shaman may use cigarette smoke to help him see what is sickening a person. The smoke augments the shaman's breath, his heart, his power. Smoke literally makes the invisible (breath, heart, and power) visible. Other medicine tools include owl or eagle feathers, rock crystals, and brushes or whips made from horse or cow hair, plants, or deer tail. The shaman uses such tools for diagnosis, whereas ritual curers use them to cure the patient.

A shaman conducts one of two diagnostic forms: a brief one called the *kulañmad* and a long version used for a more difficult or problematic diagnosis, known as a *duajida*.

Wandering sickness *(oimeliḍdam mumkidag)*, such as the flu, colds, tuberculosis, and diabetes mellitus, is not unique to the O'odham, since all humans can potentially contract these diseases. Despite the universal applicability of wandering sicknesses, they also have a mythic origin. These sicknesses wander indiscriminately over the entire planet, making all people sick. Unlike staying sicknesses, however, neither shamans nor ritual curers, and therefore no songs, are called for in the treatment of these ailments. Today, one is likely to visit an Anglo physician *(milgan ma:kai)* at a clinic for the diagnosis and treatment of a wandering sickness. Shamans often make referrals to their biomedical counterparts if the shaman is unable to help their patients.

Sorcery *(hiwhoi)* is yet another condition that shamans treat diagnostically. While sorcery is neither a staying nor a wandering sickness, it can be described as a nonsickness sickness because it does produce illness-like symptoms. Only a shaman can identify or see *(ñeid)* a sorcery object in a patient's body or in their living environment (e.g., house, corral, vehicle). During a diagnosis, the shaman invokes his or her seeing capacity to discover if a patient has been ensorcelled. In fact, during a diagnosis it is as possible, if not as likely, that a shaman will discover sorcery as that he will discover a staying sickness. Sorcery objects are described variously as hot coals, horse hairs, a nail wrapped in thread, or small feathers that are magically shot into a victim's body. These objects may also be planted in the living area of the victim, in or near the house or house compound, or even in the victim's car or truck. The sorcery object grows in strength (not dissimilar to the properties of staying sicknesses) and kills the victim if it goes undetected and untreated. The sorcery object is located through the seeing of a shaman, who then sucks the object out of the body, or it is physically removed from the living area or vehicle. The object is shown to the victim before being disposed of in a can, which is later burned and buried by the shaman to destroy the evil and perhaps reverse the sorcerer's malice back upon the sorcerer himself. No curing songs are used to treat the victim of this malevolence. While anyone is capable of sorcery, it is an evil shaman (*pi-ap ma:kai,* literally, "no good shaman") who is most often suspected and implicated in sorcery accusations.

Because of a shaman's power, the prevalence of interpersonal envy, and the pervasive threat of sorcery, there is a universal fear of and profound respect for the shaman. This is because any power an individual may possess to do good deeds (diagnosis and cure) may also be used for diabolical or self-serving ends.

DL: It is between the good and the bad. For instance, people think it's good, in a good health way, that shamans help their people by diagnosing and curing them. And to the bad ones, *pi-ap mamakai,* it's caused by something like jealousy or envy. But shamans are good. They are going to help people in a good way. At the same time they can be bad. They know bad spells to put on other people who they don't like, and they will make them sick. A person who doesn't like a medicine man and gets too rough with him, or if a person is too fancy, and shows off, then the shaman can get mad at them.

At times they help people pretty good, and they see people in a nice way. But if you bother a shaman, and you are the one who is angering them, well that's when they get mad at you. They could do just anything bad to you, whatever they want to do. And they'll throw it behind your back without letting you know, and you won't realize it until you get sick. But at times a medicine man will even say it right to your face: "You are going to be dead at this time. You are going to be gone that day. You are mean to me, and you're going to be gone that year. I'm going to do this to you."

When a person becomes a medicine man, things just come to them in their dreams. And even when they're just kids, their medicine-man elders do or give something to them, but they don't say that "you're going to be a good shaman, you're going to be a bad medicine man." They just do something to them, and it's up to the person when they grow up which way they are going to go. Are they going to be a good medicine man, or are they going to be a bad medicine man? "Am I going to help, or am I going to harm people? Or am I just going to be in between?"

So all that is not bad, it's just in between the good and bad. It isn't up to a person; it just happens when they're a kid or later in their dreams. A person's elders, when they die, they will do something for their younger kids, like for their granddaughter or grandson or other close relative. They think to themself, "Oh, I'm going to die now, and I'm going to throw this power and give it to the next one so they become a medicine man or lady. But I don't know which way they'll go Will they be a good medicine lady or a good medicine man? That will be up to them to decide when they grow up." I guess that it just happens, and they become either a bad medicine man or a good medicine man.

But I think that some of them work pretty good. They don't go outside it; they work in between, work with people in good ways, but some hate people and work it through their bad way, *hiwhoi*.

DK: Cars, trucks, homes, livestock, refrigerators, radios, TVs, telephone poles, and even saints' images can be ensorcelled to adversely affect the well-being of the intended human victim or victims. Perhaps any material object can be ensorcelled.

Once while visiting Juan, a church leader in Covered Wells,

> he was showing me the saint images people had brought to him for repair. He said, "Look at these little holes in the paint, this is where an evil person put something [sorcery object] into that saint." He then took me to a large, near-life-size image, pointing to what looked like nail holes in the back of the image. He said, "This is the work of an evil person—they make a hole then put a horse hair or owl feather in there. That makes the person sick, the one who owns the image. They bring them to me to fix. I patch the holes and paint over them; that makes it OK again to use. Or, sometimes, the person takes it to a *ma:kai* who takes out the horse hair and burns it. If they do this, the one who put it in there will slowly turn black and die a slow death."

Saint Way: *Sa:nto Himdag*

The O'odham experienced a long and relatively amicable contact with Christianity (especially when compared to the Pueblos' catastrophic experiences). The Roman Catholic influence is visible in every O'odham village where the primary structure other than individual family homes is a native-built chapel (Griffith 1975) and in some cases a missionary-founded church (Griffith 1974). The majority of O'odham are at least nominally Catholic, although perhaps as many as 20 percent of the population now belong to a Protestant denomination. It is an understatement to say that Catholic beliefs have made a profound impact on O'odham consciousness. In fact, it is reasonable to state that O'odham religious life is largely Catholic, although it is a native folk-Catholicism.

The Jesuits brought the word of God but failed to institutionalize their version of Christianity. In fact, missionaries were absent from the region when the O'odham self-Christianized. What the O'odham developed in the latter part of the nineteenth century centered on the construction of small, family-built and -managed chapels modeled on Mexican Spanish forms, the worship of saints, and eventually the practice of five types of Christian ritual, all without resident priests: calendrical fiestas, life-crisis fiestas, wakes and funerals, death anniversaries, and All Souls observances (Bahr 1988a). Saint way or religion is derived from practices and observances in Mexico and was originally a religious complex shared by other Christianized Indians (i.e., Mayo, Tarahumara, Yaqui) of the region. Saint way was fully established sometime in the last quarter of the nineteenth century, introduced to U.S. O'odham by David Lopez's great-grandmother.

DL: I want to tell you how I have a little Yaqui blood in myself. This story also tells how we, the Papago people, got *sa:nto himdag,* our saint religion.

My dad told me that my late great-grandpa was living across the border in Mexico. He lived in a village called Yaqui-Mayo. Way back my relatives used to go out and find ranching jobs in Mexico. Anyway, my great-grandma, who was to be my grandpa's mom, went down there to find a job. She finally found a ranching job at Yaqui-Mayo. While she was living over there, she married this Yaqui man and got two kids from him: my Lopez grandpa, Juan Diaz Lopez, and my grandma, Pauline Lopez.

I was told that this Yaqui was too mean to my great-grandma. It was said that her husband fought her every time when he got drunk, and he would blame things on her that she just hadn't done. After a while some Yaqui people got together, some ladies and some of their husbands, and they said that they were going to move her and her two kids up north. So the next time that he, my great-grandpa, got drunk, they would take off. Anyway, they told her, "Well, when he gets drunk how he gets drunk, after he gets paid and just takes off for many days, well, just get yourself ready, and we'll ship you and your kids, take you as far north as we can." And so she was ready and had all of her and her kid's belongings packed. They waited. And then he got drunk like he does, and the Yaquis started bringing her and the kids north, and they go nonstop. Every now and then, they change drivers and wagon teams. They drive her, and at each village they tell the people there that "a man will be coming by asking for us, asking if we have passed by. Just tell him that you don't know. You haven't seen us." And they told each village what this man had done to her.

They keep on going, changing teams and drivers at times. And when they come to Hermosillo, and then to Magdalena, they start to hear that he had gotten sober and that he started asking around if anyone knew where his wife and kids were. The people said that they "don't know where she was at, so they can't say."

My great-grandpa had a feeling that somebody probably took her up north. So he started following them on horseback. At each village he came to, he would ask if they saw anything, but the people just say that they didn't see any wagons passing through. So the people didn't tell him that my great-grandma had come through. So he kept riding to Hermosillo and then got tired and went back to his home in Yaqui-Mayo.

The people dropped my late great-grandma over there at Magdalena, and some gave her a job at another ranch. She stayed there for I don't know how long, until someone thought that they had better move her to another village because he might be coming to look for her. So they get together again and move them to Imuris, Sonora, close to Magdalena. It's a Mexican-Papago village where they took her, and she found another ranch job. And she and her kids stayed there in Imuris until they decided to come back home to Covered Wells. At that time my grandpa Lopez was around ten years old, and my grandma was around twelve years old. And that's where they grow up, in Covered Wells. They stay over there, but they come over here to Santa Rosa to plant, garden, plow fields, and all that. And eventually my great-grandpa got married to one of the Castillos.

Well, and they say that my late great-grandma, my grandpa's mom, is the one that brought the rosary praying to the Papago, it was what she learned how to do from the Yaqui when she lived with the Yaquis. They built a little church over there at Covered Wells and put *sasantos*[4] in there, and they prayed and had ceremonials like San Juan because my late grandpa Lopez was named Juan.

I remember when he used to tell me all about his life and all of these things when I was growing up under him, when I was a small kid, when he adopted me. So this is why I have a little Yaqui blood in me, I'm part Yaqui. And this is where our saint religion comes from.

DK: Over a five-year period, the Lopez extended family of Santa Rosa graciously invited me to various folk-Catholic and traditional ceremonies. Early in my research I was interested in the commemorations of violent deaths with death memorials, crosses with flowers, votive candles, and other offerings made to the deceased (Kozak 1991; Kozak and Lopez 1991). It was obvious to me then that the O'odham used Christian symbolic forms in this and many other practices, while continuing to interpret violent deaths, at least partly, from a native cosmological standpoint. *Sa:nto himdag* successfully merged the two.

The O'odham celebration of All Souls' Day each November highlights this merger. In 1988 I attended this celebration at the Lopez family compound in Santa Rosa. David and nearly all of his siblings and many of his nephews and nieces were present. Four generations of the Lopez family participated. Preparations had been in process for several days. Tasks were assigned and completed. Perhaps most important was the visit to the cemetery and to roadside death memorials to tidy up the graves and accident sites of deceased relatives. A feast house was also prepared for a large meal for their ancestors' spirit visit later in the evening. A large table filled the room, and each ancestor had an assigned place setting of miniature dishes, where their favorite food and drink waited for them. At the north end of the room, a table was stacked with the family's saint images. Next to it was another table heaped with fresh fruits and vegetables, pastries, tamales, breads, and candy for the nourishment and enjoyment of their deceased ancestors. After sunset everyone crowded into the little dirt-floored structure to say the rosary and invite the spirit-ancestors to this annual dinner celebration. Tears were shed because of the recent and early death of David's sister from diabetic complications. As we filed out of the house, David's brother Philip picked up a broom and sat it by the door as he joked with the spirits, saying, "Here's a broom, don't forget to clean up after yourselves when you are finished eating." With this, Philip and I left the spirits to their dinner, locked the door, and joined the others in the main house to eat, talk, and joke with one another.

Devil Way: *Jiawul Himdag*

Devil way developed alongside saint way and has maintained a distinctive character. O'odham understand that, according to the Catholic way *(ka:toliga himdag)*, God and the devil are adversaries in an eternal battle for souls. O'odham devil way, while ostensibly Christian derived, is decidedly unorthodox, at least in the sense that it is a Christianity that goes unsanctioned by the Roman Catholic Church, and devil way is as native as saint way is Christian. Part of devil way's uniqueness stems from its association with shamans, who are the priestly equivalents and perhaps rivals of Catholic priests in the distinction between saint and devil ways.[5] Whereas saint way was and is about Catholic public ceremonialism, occasions for all to see and experience, devil way rites (diagnoses and cures) are performed in the privacy of the shaman's or patient's home. Saint way is church oriented and located in villages, therefore meant for all, while devil way originates from the wilderness, in or near mountains, and rites are private, away from the church, and therefore exclusionary of clergy. Whereas saint way and saints are linked to a European-based religion, O'odham devils are linked to the European instruments of capital. While saint way is how O'odham deal with the power of saints and Christ, devils are at least partly the O'odham's method of dealing with the problem of money, of acquisitive self-indulgence.

While it may be and probably is true that the O'odham had knowledge—perhaps extensive—of devils prior to 1875, we suggest that devil way did not emerge as the most prevalent way until the last quarter of the nineteenth century, when, as Bahr (1988a) has argued, the O'odham Christianized themselves. This also parallels the contention in the previous chapter that the O'odham's various cattle-ranching activities were not fully established until this period. This is an important point, since devil sickness is caused by the very instruments of capital and exchange brought about by the O'odham cattle industry.

Devils established their place alongside all other O'odham spirits. They reside in the wilderness, inside hollow mountains, and are at times encountered out in the desert or in dreams at home. Devils are part of the human community life in a unique manner, even though humans and devils live apart. Devils select the humans with whom they wish to communicate in order to give their power to or cause sickness in humans. In comparison, saints are housed, and therefore live, in villages inside O'odham-built chapels, missionary-built churches, roadside shrine-chapels, death memorials, on home altars, and in heaven (Kozak 1991; Kozak and Lopez 1991).

Heg wepo mat hab a
masma hab cu'ig mañ wenog,
Mo g e-matp hab cu'ig gḍ
hu'i, back in the 1920s,
mat hab mat wenog
hab-a e:p cu'ig ḍ hu'i,
tp mac wenog pi koi
anhu heḍa'i ha'icug,
ṣ t-ge'egeḍaj,
t-wosibaḍ,
c has i t-ju:juñ,
wenog pi inhu heḍa'i ha'icug,
s-kekelibaḍ.
Matp wenog hab cu'ig,
e-juñim hega'i ha'icu himdag:

jiawul himdag, koko'i himdag,
c ha'icu s-ta-e:bidam,
ha'icu himdag,
c amjed heba'i ṣonwa
t-heg amjed hab i him,
idam hab abṣ kaiham
a:cim t-wehejiḍ,

O'odham, c at-p masma
hab i him wuḍ t-himdag
c wuḍ t-mumkidag,
c wuḍ has wuḍ a:ga.
Ct has ant b'o'i a:g,
wuḍ heg t-ge:sig.
C hab amjed ṣonig ḍ hu'i,
t pi-heba'i wo huhug,
pṣ hab oi himadk
idam hab i e-ju:k,
i a'ahidag,
a:cim hemajkam,
t-wecij hemajkam
t-a'aliga,
c ha-aliga o'odham himdag,

abṣ i ha'ap masma am o

It's probably just
like that time,
like it was way back,
back in the 1920s,
the way things were
way back,
at the time when
we weren't around,
not our parents,
not our late grandparents,
nor our other relatives,
those who aren't around,
our late elders.
Like it was at that time,
the way that these traditions
were done:
devil way, spirit way,
and other dangerous things,
different ways,
and that is where it started
coming from,
the elders were just listening
about ourselves, where we
came from,
us Papago, and from
there it's our tradition,
and it's our sickness,
and it's our spirit respect.
I am not sure how to say it,
but it's our sorrow.
And that's where it is from,
it won't go away,
it will keep coming,
for all time,
for all these years,
all of us people,
our young people,
our children,
and their children's Papago
tradition,
will just continue like this

himadk, c at-p abṣ am wo
himadk hab masma ha'ap,
c wuḍ o ha-mumkidag,

and will continue and will
keep on continuing like that,
and it will always be their
sickness.

Ñe, has cum jiawul
amjed pi amjed.
Hihim ko'it amjed,
o ab ha'icu i amjed hihim idam,

Look, devils don't come
from just anywhere.
They come from our dead people,
or they are from many other
things,

añ ki:k do'ag 'oidc hegam.

and they all live along those
mountains.

Ha-amjed hihim,
hegam jejawul.
Ha'ic wuḍ hegam e-ha'icu i
t-ṣoṣoiga,
ko'idag kakawiyu, haiwañ.
Ha'icu i jiawul
ha'icu i c hegam hemajkam,
matp hab amjed hihim
hegam jiawul,
ha'icu c hab in hab
ki:himag do'ag oidc,
mac an ha-a:g mo ani
ha'icug, g jejawul.
C heba'i ce:ck t-cecegid eḍa.

That's where they are from,
the devils.
Some of them were
our pets,
our dead horses, cows.
Other devils are
those people,
who all come from
the devil,
and things that live
along the mountains,
and what we say is that they're
around, the devils.
And at times they appear in our
dreams.

Heba'i e-cecegid mat heba'i hema
wo mu:, k t ha juñim, heba'i
cece ha'ic mo ha-ñeid mat o
ceṣad ce:ga-d hega'i
E-ṣoiga. Mat e-mu:ki wenog.
Tk o hega'i man hekihu ñeid,
ñ-ṣoiga heg ceṣaj hega'i
mo, hab t-juñ, o a:g mo has

They appear at times when one
of them dies, and at times some
say that they see them
riding their horse.
And here they are dead.
Something that we already saw,
my late horse that they ride,
our relations, and we say that
they

wuḍ juñ, c e-okbaḍ,
ok e-wo:sibaḍ, o e-alidag
c hekaj wuḍ a hia
t-ṣoṣoiga,
c ha'i t-ko'idag,
Matp am hihim ama'i heg wui

are related to us, our late dad,
our late grandpa, or son,
so that's why it's our
animals,
and some of our dead.
They go over there

hega'i do'ag,
g jejawul do'ag.
He, ha'icu hab e-a'aga
mac ab a'aga O'odham
mac hemu jiawul.
Na'as hab i masma hab ce:gig,
hega'i jiawul,
mo ab amjed i wu:ṣañ,
idam ha'icu doakam,
g kawiyu, haiwañ,
c mo'an t-ko:sig,
pi-ap'e wuhakid,
k masma i wuṣke
matp g jiawul.
Mat heba'i hema ko:sig,
heba'i hema ha'icu
woi i e-ce:gid:
Kawiyu hab cu'ig ha'ap
mo heba'i, heba'i wuṣke
g o'ohon.
Eḍa, mat g
kawiyu wo g o'odham mo'o-d,

hebi wo g o'odham kakiokad,
o haiwañ g o'odham mo'okaḍ,
ṣ-ge o'odham kakiokad,
o g o'odham wo
g haiwañ e-mo'okaḍ,
t g haiwañ kakiokad,
b'o mas mo'okaḍ mo g haiwañ.
C hega'i jiawul,
c hekid hab a'aga jiawul.
Ñe, ṣ hab a:c wenog hemho
pi ñeid añi wenog,
ṣ hab c hema ha'ap
e-piast hasko,
ṣ an hema ke:k o'odham
naumkam,
ṣ-hab hema him uwi s-keg
eñga,
mo hab masma eñgaḍac g u'uwi,

to that mountain,
the devil mountain.
So now there is something
in Papago
that we call devil.
In a way it was named that,
and that devil,
where it comes from,
such as all of the animals,
the horse, cow,
and in our sleep,
they don't appear too good,
and it appears
like the devil.
And in someone's sleep,
sometimes something
will appear:
The horse will appear
at times, they appear
like in the Bible.
At times,
the horse will have a human
head,
or will have human feet,
or a cow will have a human head,
human legs,
or a human will have
a cow's head,
or a cow's feet,
have a head like a cow.
And that's the devil,
and sometimes we call that devil.
Look, one time, but I didn't
see it happen,
there was a
dance somewhere,
and there was a drunk man
standing there,
and here comes a beautiful
lady with beautiful clothes,
the way the ladies are dressed,

c s-keg ha'icu e:p hab ju:kc
c s-keg hab ju:kc.
C bei hega'i ceoj,
ṣ gmhu wo e-waila,
ṣ ami him, t-hab kaidam

mo g mat hemu u'uwi hab
masma e'ñgaḍac.
Heba'i ke:k mat g ṣu:ṣk
mo g u'u:g ce:cem ṣu:ṣk.
Ṣ hab mas kaidam i hega'i,
ṣ-oi him k e-waila,
hab kaidam hega'i.
Ṣ a oia ha'i haha cegima
hab cu'ig,
k haiwañ taḍ k kakayo.
Ñe, am ipuḍ weco,
maṣ bahi am e-wiḍutahim,
hegam s-mai mat wuḍ
hega'i jiawul uwi.
Haiwañ am jiwa wui,
c hega'i naumkam waila.
Tp oia s-mai hega'i kompañloc,

k oia abṣ e-cuhugid,
cum hekid mia s-ap cu'ig ama'i.

S-ap cu'ig hema t a:g
ma:kai ama'i.
Hekaj a'agiḍ maṣ pi-woho
t wuḍ o'odham uwi:

"Hega'i wuḍ jiawul
hega'i matp am waila."
Am hia heg dagito s-cuhugam,
kt hega'i uwi gnhu huhugim,

c pi-amhu e:p e-ce:g.
E:p i:da hab e-a:g matp
wuḍ uwi,
c hab kaidam him natp hab e-a:g

and she wears fancy things
and keeps herself beautiful.
And she grabbed that man, and
they went dancing,
and when she started walking,
it sounded like
the way that the ladies
are dressed now.
Like at times their shoes
are high-heeled shoes.
And she sounded like that,
when she started to dance,
she sounded like that.
And some noticed she was
like that,
and she had cow's feet and legs.
Look, and under the dress,
her tail was swinging,
and they discovered that
she was a devil woman.
The cow came to him,
and danced with that drunk man.
Then the dancing partner found
out,
and he just fainted,
and there's always a good
medicine man nearby.
It's a good thing that there's
a medicine man around.
The shaman told the drunk man
right away that it's not a human
lady:
"The one you danced with
was a devil."
She took off into the night,
that lady took off and
disappeared,
and it didn't show up again.
And here the drunk thought it
was a human lady,
and she sounds and walks like

mo hekaj je:kc ṣu:ṣk	she has on
mo g u'uk ce:cem.	high-heeled shoes.
Ṣ-eḍa hega'i haiwañ hu:cic	And here the cow hooves
kakkio c heg hab kaidam him.	and legs sound like that.
Tp oia m ha'i ha'icu an i	And some people found out and
e-a'agiḍ am i, e-kai,	told each other, and she overheard,
o g am dagito,	and she let that drunk man go,
k kompañloc hema	and sometimes a dancing partner
kt hega'i jiawul	like that devil
uwi masma am i e-cecegiḍ t-wui.	woman will appear to someone.
Kaij hemajkam ha'i ama'i,	It does that to any human,
g cecegiḍ am o	the devil will
moḍ hega'i jiawul	show itself
cum heba'i ceoj, uwi,	anywhere to a man, lady,
o g ali—	or child—
wui g ali wui abṣ cum has	it will go toward them in just
masma.	this way.

The sacred landscape of Native Americans has received increased academic attention of late, perhaps spurred by the conflicts over sacred sites such as Mount Graham in Arizona or Blue Lake in New Mexico. Mountains tend to be a very important part of the sacred landscape. There are several sacred mountains in the O'odham creation story. Perhaps most important is Baboquivari (Waw Giwulk, or Constricted Rock), where a cave is known as the home of their man-god creator, I'itoi. Others are Greasy Mountain, south of Phoenix, and Superstition Mountain, southeast of Phoenix. These mountains are discussed in the origin story and are the locations of important events in the creation of the O'odham as a people. Other aspects of sacred place, both natural and human made, include the ocean (Gulf of California), the Colorado River, the Children's Shrine, Where-the-Ceremonial-Runner-is-Buried (Nawicu Hiaṣpañ), and the Witch's Cave, near the *ejido* of Poso Verde, Mexico. Combined, these locations serve as identifiers of place, locations that both remind and teach the O'odham about who they are and their place in the world.

Devil mountains are also sacred locations found in the Sonoran Desert. Not destinations for individual or community pilgrimages, devil mountains are rather the destinations of O'odham who were cowboys during their lifetime. Each devil mountain stands in a cattle-ranching range, and they are located away from but usually adjacent to inhabited villages. It is probably true that every human village has a nearby devil mountain. In this way, each village has its own afterlife location for some of its deceased ancestors.

DL: So all these devil mountains are similar. The cowgirls live in one part, and the cowboys live in the other part. And when somebody gets sick, just like over here at Chui Chu, this man got sick, got real sick, and in his dreams the devils took him over there to this mountain near Chui Chu. And I guess they're the same, the mountains. And the devils took him over there, showed him what they do there.

The devils said, "Look at all of this here; this is where us cowboys live. Look at what we do here. We like to do this because it's our favorite job, roping and riding wild horses—just like on the open range."

It looks big to them, and here it's just a little mountain. And here the devil's home in the mountain is just like where us Papago live in the desert.

That sick man said, "Then somebody wanted to saddle a horse and start riding, but it bucked and ran all the way around inside that mountain before it came back, and here it's a good-sized mountain." And the devil said to the sick man, "Wait here until you see the next thing, I'm going to show you the next part of the mountain."

So then the devil took him to another part of the mountain and said, "This is where the cowgirls live." And the devil cowgirls were doing the same thing. And it seems like it's just a wide-open big village, and here it's just inside a little devil mountain.

So that's how the devils live. It's just like we do here, except that it's just in a little mountain. But they live like we do. They have wagons and horses, and they have corrals and roping pens.

So the devil tried to tell that man to choose something that he wanted to use. There were bridles, spurs, saddles, and all that cowboy stuff. He tried to tell the man to pick up something. The sick man said to me, "But I didn't really pick up anything, the only thing I picked up was a lariat, a cowhide lariat, a rope. The only thing that I picked up was that. Then I woke up, and I found out I was sleeping on my bed. Here it was just in my dream.

The man said, "So, this is why I don't really know very much about cowboying, but if I had picked up something real important I might be a better cowboy now, or even a medicine man. But it's not up to me. I just picked up that little lariat, and now I'm a good cowboy; I can rope and all that. But I didn't find anything [shamanic knowledge] from that."

DK: I was warned at different times and by different people about my commuting past Roughrock Mountain (S-hiwk Do'ag), near Chui Chu in the northern part of the Sells reservation. The highway that passes this mountain is lined with death memorials, crosses marking the place where a person died in a car accident (Kozak 1991). Some call this stretch of highway the Valley of Death.

In August 1992 I was visiting with Enoch and Rose Thomas of Chui Chu village. Rose had recently been released from the hospital after breaking her arm in an auto accident. We were discussing why there are so many death memorials along the reservation roads south of Chui Chu. Rose said, "I'm not sure, but something is going on there. At different times Enoch and I have seen things, you know, along that road. They [devils] are all over that road and mountain. One second they are there, and the next they are gone." Enoch agreed. He said, "One time we were driving over there at night, and Rose said that there were some lights up on the mountain, and there are no roads up there. I started driving really fast to get past it. I don't like that place. Rose got out her holy water that she carries with her, and she crossed herself." Rose added, "I cross myself every time we drive by that mountain where the crosses are; we both do that." After a long pause she continued: "I wonder why no one has done anything about this. It would be good if some people would build a little house for a saint, like for the Virgin, and a cross—devils don't like the cross. Maybe they'd stop bothering people. You be careful driving there down to Santa Rosa, especially at night."

Unconsciousness

O'odham culture is known in the literature as a "dream culture" in that nocturnal dreams provide individuals with personal power.[6] While dreaming is not an intentional method of power acquisition, there were three active, though now moribund, forms of power acquisition among the O'odham. Underhill (1946) reports that the killing of an enemy (Apache), killing an eagle, and making a pilgrimage to the ocean for salt served as individual quests for power. Each method of power getting involved and required dreaming.

Devils and other spirits approach intoxicated persons because they are not fully conscious. However, drunkenness is not the only altered form of consciousness that stimulates a spirit's visit. Spirits appear to people who are asleep, delirious with a sickness, in a coma, or knocked unconscious. There is a substantial folklore about people who are knocked unconscious by horses. It is said that if a horse knocks a person unconscious, devils often appear to take that person on a journey to a devil's mountain abode. We have heard many stories of cowboys who were bucked off of their horses, knocked unconscious in the fall, and then approached by horse-riding devils. Each of the tellings follows a pattern similar to that of a story told to Underhill (1946, 287) sixty years earlier: "I once fell from a horse and was unconscious for twenty-four hours. During that time, devils came to me. . . . They were riding horses and had a spare horse for me. We rode inside the mountain ranges and saw the gold and silver piled up there. They sang and I learned their songs. When I came to, I was singing them."

The folklorist Kathleen Sands in her work with the late Theodore Rios recorded an excellent example of the devil-lore genre in 1974 in Sells, Arizona:

> And the way I heard this story, it happened like that. He saddled a horse. It's kind of wild horse. When he got on, that horse bucked him off. Laying there unconscious, he don't know nothing, but it's the time when those fellows came out, when he was unconscious. He knew that some guys came around, took him up, told him, "Go with us. We'll take you." Set him on another horse.
>
> Off they went, gallop, right straight on. Two of them I guess, one on each side. They just went—some hill down there, some black, dark hill. And they were going right straight in towards it. Just about the time they're reaching it, it opened. They just went right in there, in that hill. There it is—everything was there. It's a big castle or something.
>
> "Here we are."
>
> "Yeah."

"Look around and see what you like."

He looks around. Everything was there: spurs, bridles, silver, saddles, whatever. And there were horses, good horses. And they try to ask him if he can ride one. "No, I can't." And it happened like that. Well, they show him around, all the way. I don't know how long, but finally they say, "Well, I think if you want to go we'll take you."

"Okay, I want to go."

"But, we'll give you some medicine first, a drink of something, before you go." But this we are going to give you, *you're going to be just like a good one*." He don't know what they meant by "good one" but he says, "All right." So they dish him out a glass of whatever it was, a bowl or whatever. And he drinks whatever it was. "Take it, take all of it. If you can, take all of it. Drink it all at once." Took it, and he tasted it some way—I don't know how—but he was drinking, drinking. Before he got it all, he felt it was BLOOD. Turned around—some left, still some left. It was BLOOD.

"You didn't drink it."

"Oh, no, that's all I want to drink." He knew it was BLOOD. "Why don't you drink it all?"

"No, I can't." He wouldn't drink it. "Okay." And then while he was leaving, he was leaving they told him, "Since you didn't drink all that, when anybody's sick like that you won't be able to cure him as well, whether he'd dead, half dead, for the reason you didn't drink it all. If you had drunk it all up, well, you'd heal better than that. So if you want to go, go ahead." Picked out a gold piece, brick, gold. "Take it home." He went.

Then when he was coming, "Why am I carrying this? I'm not supposed to be carrying it." Threw it away. That gold piece. And then, finally, when he came to, he was right in that corral, in that corral where he was bucked off. He was still there, out in the sun. Nobody around. Nobody around. He got up, thought about the horse. Horse was over eating grass, saddle on, everything, when he got up.

So, there it is. From then on, he started as a medicine man. He knew it then that he was a medicine man. But it happened like that. Them were the devils that took him. (Kathleen Sands, tape transcription in her possession)

Underhill and Rios's stories, although recorded over three decades apart, have much in common and reveal a continuity in devil belief over those years. And twenty years after Rios's rendition, we have both listened to similar devil-visit accounts.

DL:

Na'as hab e-wua,	The way it happened,
masma hab e-wua mat	the way it happens when
g hemajkam wuḍ t-naumk,	somebody gets drunk,
mat heba'i wo hema	at times a person
e-ge:sid g hemajkam,	will pass out,
wo si naumk wo e-ge:sid hasko,	will get really drunk and will pass out somewhere,
o'om e-ki: am o gmhu abṣ	even in his own home or out
hasko,	anywhere else,
o matk hema wo mumku,	or if someone is sick,
wo si mumku,	will be very sick,
o cum hems abṣ kosc-oḍ.	or even if a person is just napping or asleep.
G jiawul wo wui jiwa,	The devil will approach him,
mat wo ha'icu maṣca,	will teach or train him,
o abṣ am wo i e-ce:g wo	or will just appear and
mumkic,	make him sick,
o hascu abṣ a:g am wo i e-	or just anything can happen
ce:g,	when they arrive,
abṣ ha'icu a:g am wo i e-	they will just appear for any
ce:g,	old reason,
pegi abṣ o s-ñeidam,	maybe they just want to see,
o abṣ mumkicud am.	or just want to make him sick.
Hekaj am wo i e-ce:g	That's one way they will
abṣ cum has masma	appear, just anyway,
cum has wuḍ wo naumk,	even if one is drunk,
o pi eḍ wo naumk, abṣ	or not drunk,
wo ko'i,	just sleeping,
o mumkudam cum has i masma,	or is sick in some way,
ba wenog hab si e-wua	but it really happens
mapt wuḍ o naumk,	when you are drunk,
c wo e-ge:sid wenog,	and will be passed out,
am wo i e-ce:g.	and that's when they will appear.

DK: That drunkenness in O'odham society leads to spirit visits is not surprising. The ethnographic record is full of references to the functional and communal importance of ritual alcohol consumption in O'odham society, for instance, the annual rain dance and sit-and-drink (Crosswhite 1980; Underhill 1946; Waddell 1975).

> Interpretations of these rituals say that alcohol consumption invites rain clouds to the desert, strengthens ties between widely scattered kinsmen, and reaffirms an egalitarian ethos between them (Waddell 1976, 222–26). Notably, a rain shaman meets with spirits to discover when the rains will arrive. Along with but apart from communal drunkenness, individuals at the rain dance or sit-and-drink may also be approached by spirits.
>
> In other secular drinking contexts, Waddell (1975) discusses individual drinking as a source of what he calls "social credit." He suggests that drinking with others is a way to mediate economic and social differences between individuals. The giving and accepting of alcoholic drinks is central to the attainment of good-will between peers because it maintains equality between persons. Failure to share drinks is perhaps shameful, and alcohol consumption, according to Waddell, lubricates social interactions that are fraught with uncertainty and ambiguity.

We suggest that various states of unconsciousness have a symbolic affinity to the death state.[7] That unconsciousness equals symbolic death is revealed with an etymological analysis of the three O'odham definitions of the intransitive verb *mu:*. Its most common meaning is "to die" (*ko'i* is the plural form). But *mu:* can also mean "to become paralyzed," as in the sentence, "Abṣ i mu: g ñ-cu:kug," "I am paralyzed," or literally, "My body just died." *Mu:* has the additional meaning of "to faint," "to pass out," as in the clause, *Ṣopol mu:,* "He passed out," or literally, "He died for a short time." The latter two meanings reveal that when the human body is not animated and lacks conscious awareness, as in any unconscious state, the body is metaphorically and symbolically dead. Passing out from an alcohol-induced intoxication, being knocked unconscious by a horse, or merely sleeping safely and soundly in one's bed bring a person to a condition analogous to death, a state that predisposes a living human to an approach by spirits.

It is in any one of these unconscious states that the physical, sentient body is in a sense no longer a hindrance to meeting with a spirit. However, unconsciousness is not the only criterion and is perhaps of minor importance in meeting a spirit, because a spirit visit always occurs on the spirit's terms; that is, living humans only interact with spirits when the spirit decides to take a human to its home, or show or teach the human something. The spirit makes this decision if it believes that a living human is a worthy recipient, which is at least partly based on the human's learning of songs from other humans. For instance, if a person knows many devil songs and sings them with pride and a strong voice, a devil or devils might in the future give that person new and individualized devil songs, because the devils, like other spirit tutelaries, are prideful and enjoy hearing about themselves. The spirit is proud of its unique and, at times, quirky attributes, so singing the songs of spirits endears the human to the spirit and opens the way for future communications.

The Problems of Wealth and Envy

The conspicuous display of wealth is the prerogative of devils. Whereas devils are universally known by O'odham to be dressed in the finest clothing and jewelry, and to be rich *(s-kakais),* many say that humans should never overtly display their wealth. To do so is considered shameless self-aggrandizement and is frowned upon by other O'odham. Displaying one's wealth is considered poor taste and is viewed as setting oneself above and apart from one's community members and social obligations. It suggests excessive self-indulgence and is analogous to cynically rubbing another's face in one's own good fortune. Wealth differences arouse the envy and jealousy of any person who sees this flaunting, and it is foolish to raise the ire and envy of others precisely because it may lead to sorcery. A rich person who shows off, flaunts his material success, runs the risk of supernatural sanction and harm from an envious shaman or sanctions from neighbors.

Devils, on the other hand, are not subject to these human constraints. Some devils are rich and flaunt their wealth in a way that a living human never should. Devils are, in fact, assumed to be rich in a way that humans never are. This presents a problem for wealthy cattle ranchers, who are often the targets of sorcery.

Lopez is familiar with and Kozak has heard other accounts of people who hire an evil shaman *(pi-ap ma:kai)* to ensorcell a rich person in order to "ruin" the person—his health, wealth, or both.

DL:

Na'as ama s-wohom	I think that it's true
s-hab a cu'ig moḍ jiawul.	that it [wealth] is devil like.

Heg hekaj mo hega'i mo ha'icu
mac an hekihu hab a'aga lial,
c idam s-kakais mo
hab cu'ig s-haiwañga.
Ṣ hab-a pi has cu'ig
mo pt wuḍ o s-kaiskaḍ,
wo s-haiwañga,
aba s-ap wo hekaj!
Hega'i lial,
mapt pi amhu
s-mu'i amhu wo to'akjiḍ,
abṣ s-ba:bagai hekaj,
s-ap wo hekaj,
am o ha'ic cece
e:p idam o'odham,
ha'ic he s-hehegam
hab o wo cu'ig
hab s-haiwañ, c hekid hema
taṣkaj ñeiḍ m-abṣ
hi ha-gaggaḍa
g e-haiwañga mu'i am to'akjiḍ
g lial mu'i ñekeḍ k e-lialga.
Mu'i u'ahim g lialga,
"Nt am hig o a:g g ma:kai
t-am has o ṣa ju:
hega'i o'odham,
k ab o ṣopolkad g haiwañga.

O am has wo ṣa ju:,
pi anhu ha'icug."
Kt heba'i g ma:kai
hejel pi-ap ma:kai,

hejel hab i e-a'aga
"N-ḍo has ṣa ju: k hega'i
o'odham wo s-ta ṣo'igcud,
abṣ s e-gimaihun
g e-lialga amjed,
c ha'icu e'eñga amjed ha'ic."
Hab cu'ig mo hia woho
moḍ s-kakais,

That's because of something
we already said about money,
and those who are rich and
who possess many cows.
But it doesn't really
matter that you'll be rich,
and will possess many cows,
but use them the right way!
That money,
you don't have to
keep a lot of money,
just use it slowly,
carefully, the right way,
because at times some say
these people,
some are jealous that the
rich have
too many cows, and sometimes
we see someone just selling
their cows and will be just
hoarding a lot of their money,
carrying a lot of money.
Someone will say,
"I'll tell a medicine man
to do something
about that person,
and we'll reduce the number of
his cows.
I'll just do something,
and they won't be around."
And at times the shaman
is himself a no-good medicine
man,
and will think to himself,
"I will do something
so that person will be poor,
because that person is just
showing off with his money,
and with his belongings."
It's true about some
of the rich people,

c abṣ e:sto hekaj e-lialga,	and they just use money kind of hidden,
c ha'icu e'ẽnga ha'ic,	and their expensive belongings,
hab cu'ig mat am	so that way they
wo al ha'i hekaj	will just use a few and
pi-ap ṣo b'o'e'elid,	will not think to themself,
"Añi wuḍ s-kais, c	"I'm rich, and I
s-haiwañga,"	have a lot of cows,"
p ṣam ha-ce:gid hemajkam ha-	and he will be showing off to
wui,	the people,
mo p si ha-gagda k e-haiwañga,	and he will be selling a lot of his cows,
ha'icu s-keg ha'icu u'u-him,	and will be buying expensive things,
c hekid jiawul hega'i	and the devil
hekaj pi ab we:mt,	won't help him,
ṣ has cu'ig e:p jiawul	that devil when
tp mapt wuḍ o s-kaisga-d.	you are rich.
Hab-a am haba e:p cu'ig	But it's the same thing that
jiawul hab ha'icu juñim,	the devil is doing,
k mat wo mumkic g hemajkam,	and he will make people sick,
o om has wo i ju: t-wo ṣo'ig	or do something about it and will make poor
g hemajkam m abṣ i	that human who's just showing
e-gimaihun e-hemajkam ha-wui	off toward the people
mo ṣo'igcud.	who are poor.
C hekaj hegam ṣo'igkam	And that's why
hemajkam heba'i	the poor people sometimes
hema hab i e-a'aga,	think,
"N-do hema behi g ma:kai,"	"I'll hire a shaman,"
o hejel wuḍ o ma:kai, "N-do	or if he's a shaman himself he'll say, "I'll treat
si ju: hega'i o'odham s gimai,	that person who is showing off,
k eliḍ mo s-lialga eḍa,	and here he thinks he has lots of money,
c woho ṣa'i lialga,	and it's true that he has much money,
am b'o ju: hega'i jiawul cikpan,	and we'll do the devil's job,
hekaj wuḍ woho jiawul hega'i."	cause he's truly a devil."

DK: It is a reasonable hypothesis to suggest that O'odham devil way is a pointed response to and critique of the Jesuit and later the Franciscan Christian indoctrination. It is clear that O'odham accepted the idea that the devils the priests talked about were themselves. It was they who were accused of being sinful humans, and as such at death they were to go to hell with the devil. Christianity challenged the O'odham afterlife location of *si'alig weco,* where humans became owls *(cukuḍ)* at death. Presently, with Christian influence, some of their dead become devils who inhabit a new land of the dead, close by but still removed from the living. That O'odham are devils themselves suggests a kind of acceptance that is similar to the findings of Taussig's (1987) study of the Putumayo Indians of Colombia, South America, where the spirits of the dead, of the ancient ones, are perceived by today's shamans as sorcerers, and where shamans are perceived as "devils" in their own right.

Why this acceptance occurred is not at all clear. Allow me, however, to speculate on this intriguing question.

The idea of devils—where they live, how they live, what they do, and how they interact with living humans—is linked to missionization. The O'odham like the idea of the devil as the opposite of the Catholic saint. It is analogous to the dichotomy of profane humans and sacred saints. In heaven and *si'alig weco,* things are pretty good, and what people lacked in life is provided there in abundance. Both are idyllic and attractive locations or destinations. Nothing changes, however, and nothing excitingly different happens.

On the other hand, devils have all kinds of fun and excitement in their mountain homes, and they too have everything they might want or need. It is not, therefore, a bad place to be. It is not modeled after the Christian notion of hell as a place of fire, agony, and eternal damnation. While there are no Indian saints, there are plenty of Indian devils who have found homes in various devil mountains. They form a special kind of residence alongside but separate from both heaven above and *si'alig weco.* It may even be that the devils' afterlife destination is more appealing than the other two options.

Furthermore, the O'odham at least partly incorporated the devil image as they did as a critique of the missionary's abundant lifestyle. Missionaries had everything supplied to them, and they got Indians to work for them. They were never in want of anything: they had good horses, cattle, clothing, and sexual access to Indian women—a description of missionary life that is not dissimilar to the description of the devils' mountain homes and lives. Missionaries planted the notion of devils in their hearts and minds and instilled the idea that they (particularly O'odham shamans) were devils or at least the worshipers of pagan, non-Christian deities. Devils did not become gods for the O'odham—devils were merely themselves. It was only after death that O'odham reaped the material goods of the earthly realm—both a Christian and native conceptualization. Wealth in the human world came to symbolize ill-gotten material goods—gotten just as unfairly as missionaries had obtained them.

It is this image that is recreated in devil-lore, an afterlife image attainable only in dreams and death. The image is simultaneously a critique of missionary Christianity in that O'odham accepted devils as themselves without attaching the stigma that the devil held for the missionaries. But it is also a critique of the missionary's excessive control of scarce resources. It is conceivable, if this hypothesis is correct, that the O'odham thought of missionaries as the "king devils," the "cattle barons." Moreover, early Catholic missionaries may have been the prototype of O'odham devil phantasms.

The "sin" that devil-lore speaks to and admonishes people for is self-serving behavior at the expense of the community good. One should not be wealthy in the face of others' want because it indicates that one's excessive gains are achieved through dubious means.

This hypothetical reconstruction emphasizes how the Christian devil was adopted but its original Christian meanings inverted. Missionaries themselves were devils, the owners of large herds. They were the original "king devils" that devil-lore describes. But O'odham also thought of themselves as devils, particularly those who were excessively concerned with wealth. By accepting that devils were themselves, that devils were not necessarily evil, and that devil mountains became an acceptable, perhaps even desirable afterlife destination, they inverted the missionary's theologically based claim that the O'odham were devils, evil, and needing salvation. In a sense, they were merely seeking that which the missionaries already possessed—access to material wealth and possessions to satisfy their needs.

4

Jiawul Mumkidag: Devil Sickness

> **And we'll see the medicine man,**
> **and he'll say,**
> **"The devils are making you sick."**
> **And he means about the devils that reach us.**

Devil sickness is probably today's most frequently diagnosed staying sickness, and every O'odham is in one way or another susceptible to it. Cowboys, however, are particularly prone to it, though anyone who has direct contact with cattle and horses is at risk. In any case, sickness is the result of a person being disrespectful to a horse or a cow, the devils' property. Disrespect takes the form of physically abusing livestock or looking at them in an inappropriate manner. It is also disrespectful for a pregnant woman to watch the slaughter of a cow.

Once a person begins to experience the symptoms of an illness, family members urge them to seek medical help. A shaman is contacted to diagnose the illness or problem. If the diagnosis is relatively straightforward, then it will be accomplished in the briefer *kulañmaḍ* (to look for illness). It may only last an hour or two, the time that it takes a shaman to identify the sickness-causing spirit or the sorcery object. In any case, this diagnostic session can take place during the day. We attended the following diagnosis in the summer of 1993. It was apparently unproblematic, hence its brevity.

DK: He lights up a Camel cigarette. Sitting five feet away, the *ma:kai* blows billowing clouds of blue smoke over his patient, who sits quietly and calmly on the edge of a bed. A tin can rests on a little table to his right, where the *ma:kai* carefully places the cigarette ashes. He inhales deeply on the cigarette, holds the smoke for a moment, and then slowly exhales. Each exhalation covers the patient from head to toe. After smoking about half of the cigarette, he quietly snuffs it out. All conversation ceases between the *ma:kai* and the others present. The *ma:kai* rises, approaches the patient, and begins to touch him gently, making small invisible crosses on the patient's chest, forehead, temples, shoulders, back, arms, wrists, thighs, shins, and finally the tops of his feet. All the while he recites a prayer in O'odham.

The *ma:kai* goes to the side of the room, where he keeps three feather fans in separate three-pound Folgers coffee tins. He selects the one with the longest feathers (eagle) and caresses them gently. He uses the feathers to fan the patient and the air around him. The feather tips lightly touch the patient. He begins the fanning at the patient's chest, works on his face and head, and goes down the back to his arms. At his arms the *ma:kai* allows the feathers to beat in rapid, audible succession. Occasionally he stops, spits on the feather tips, and then resumes the fanning. Some of the saliva hits the patient. After pausing at the patient's arms, the *ma:kai* finishes the round at the patient's feet. All the while he mumbles a barely audible prayer, and all the while the patient is silent.

The *ma:kai* returns the eagle feather fan to its coffee tin. Sliding his chair close to the patient, he picks up the patient's left forearm and begins to massage. Working from the shoulder he moves quickly to the wrist, which he squeezes between his hands until it makes a barely audible crack. The *ma:kai* stands up and begins to gulp air and belch. After several minutes of this, he leans toward his patient and begins blowing and sucking on the patient's left arm. The *ma:kai* periodically spits into the can where he put the cigarette ashes. The sucking sacrament continues for about ten minutes.

The *ma:kai* sits back down. He reports to all present what is making his patient sick. It is the devils. Devils apparently knocked the person down, which caused the wrist injury. He reports that he has returned the wrist to its proper position. The *ma:kai* then asks the patient if he wants to have the blood vessels returned to their proper positions. These were misaligned in the "accident." The patient answers with a nod and *heu'u,* yes.

The *ma:kai* rises and goes to a table on the side of the room opposite from where he keeps his feather fans. On this table stand a few saints' images, some holy water, a votive candle, variously colored ribbons, a basket, and a pack of Camel cigarettes. He returns with a small cup in his hand, filled with holy water. While saying another prayer, the shaman dabs his fingers in the water and crosses the patient with them. He again follows the same path on the patient's body: chest, head, back, and eventually his feet. When he reaches the patient's left wrist, he pays special attention. Here he traces four straight eight-inch lines on the top of the patient's forearm with the holy water. Over and over he traces the blood vessels. Over and over he makes the sign of the cross at the exact location of the injury.

After completing this, the *ma:kai* gives his patient instructions for the following weeks. First, eat no meat, salt, or anything red for the next twenty-four hours. Second, do not do any heavy work or lifting for the next six weeks. Strenuous activity will aggravate the problem. Third, do not sleep with your wife for the next six nights because she might roll over and reinjure the wrist. The diagnosis *(kulañmaḍ)* is complete.

Difficult diagnoses require more lengthy diagnostic sessions, which are called the *duajida* (literally, to cure), in which the shaman must obtain his spirit helper's assistance in diagnosis. In either the short or long diagnosis, a shaman will have his patient hire singers who know the songs for their cure.

Defining Devil Sickness

Defining devil sickness, or any other staying sickness, is not easy. Symptoms do not tell the entire story. Shamans, who are best equipped to define a staying sickness, are also the least likely to attempt an explanation. It seems to us that a single, authoritative definition of staying sickness is elusive because it may be an undertheorized subject for shamans and the O'odham theory of sickness and cure. If nothing else, the shaman's process of defining a patient's sickness is imbued with mystical overtones, and his knowledge is not made publicly available. Our definition of devil sickness, therefore, is not as complete as we would wish.

While sorcery is implicated in the devil phenomenon, devil sickness is most commonly contracted by cowboys who are disrespectful toward their animals. Devil sickness is closely linked to the cattle industry. It may be an important service in that it prescribes the appropriate behavior toward, and checks and limits the poor treatment of, horses and cattle. The behavioral constraints of devil sickness are therefore like other staying sickness ways, which all assure respectful thoughts and provide behavioral proscriptions toward the spirit entity and its earthly representatives.

DL:

Hega'i jiawul mumkidag,	That devil sickness,
mo a'aga a:cim, g o'odham,	what it means to us, the Papago,
mat ha'icu o t-mumkic,	when something makes us sick,
masma mo heba'i mat g ma:kai	like at times, when a shaman
hab wo cei jejawul	says that devils
mat wo t-mumkic,	will sicken us,
mat wo s-ko'okam t-ju:,	that they will hurt us,
o ab has wo t-ju:,	or do something to us,
kawiyu ab haiwañ ab,	from the horse or cow,
wuḍ t-melickwa o t-wua,	they run over us and knock
wo t-mo'ockwa,	us down, or horn us,
ok wijina wo t-ge:k,	or if a rope hits us,
o om has i juñ ha'icu mo in	or if anything happens, like at
hab t-wuihim wapkial ab o	times it just happens when cowboying or
abṣ cum hascu mo heba'i	just anything, like at times
g ha'icu, abṣ	just something
na:nko abṣ s-ta juñim.	odd will occur.
T wo ñeid ma:kai t b o cei,	And we'll go see a medicine man, and he'll say,
"Mat g jiawul mumkic"	"That devil is making you sick,"
heg hab a'aga hega'i	and he means that
mo g jejawul wo t-a'ahepaḍ,	the devils will reach us, and
mat hemho o wa t-wuso	that we will have to cure
g jiawulkaj,	from the devils,
heba'i hema hab cece,	and at times one will say,

"Haiwañkaj wo t-wuso,"
o heba'i hema hab cece,
"Mat k cukuḍkaj wo t-wuso
no pi g wuḍ a ha'i
wuḍ a ha'i hegam
jejawul-cu:ckuḍ."
T heba'i hema hab wo cei
mat g "kawiyukaj
wo t-wuso mat g heba'i
kawiyu wo i t-wua,
wuḍ hega'i jiawul ñeñe'i
wesig,
haiwañ ñeñe'i, kawiyu ñeñe'i,
c eḍa wes hegam jiawul
ñeñe'i. Mac hegam amjed
hab a'aga mo hega'i
wuḍ jiawul mumkidag,
hega'i matp heba'i wo t-a'ahe,
t ab wo cei g ma:kai mat
"g jejawul m-mumkic."
Wes heg ge:wṣpp,
cukuḍ, o kawiyu, o g haiwañ,
hemho wa mat g, c
kawiyu bahikaj wo t-wusot,
o g haiwañ bahikaj wo t-wusot,
o g cukuḍ a'ankaj wo t-wusot,
ṣ hab-a mat wuḍ o

jiawul cukuḍ mo hab a'aga,
ṣ hab-a eḍa
an hab-a cu'ig ñeñe'i.
C eḍ an hab cece g moḍ
jiawul,
a'aga wuḍ hega'i
jiawul mumkidag.

"We will cure from the cow,"
or one will say,
"We'll cure from the owl
because that is related
to the
devil-owls."
One will say that
"the horse
will cure us" when the
horse bucks us off,
and these that cure are all
devil songs,
cow songs, and horse songs,
and they are all devil songs.
So this
is what we say
about the devil sickness,
that at times devils will reach us,
and the shaman will say that
"the devils are making you sick."
It's all connected together,
owl, horse, or cow,
definitely, and
horse tail will cure,
or cow tail will cure,
or owl feather will cure,
but only if it is a sickness
caused by
the devil-owl like they say,
and it is also in
the songs.
The lyrics talk about the
devil in there,
saying that it is the
devil sickness.

Contracting Devil Sickness

As with all O'odham staying sicknesses, devil sickness is characterized by distinct physical symptoms that an afflicted person complains about to other family members. Devil sickness differs from other staying sicknesses in that the method of contagion is through direct physical contact between a human and the sickness-causing agent, a horse or a cow.

DL:

Ñe, hega'i jiawul mumkidag,	Look, that devil sickness,
mat g kawiyu wo m-keihi	when a horse kicks you,
mo hab a:g mo mas heg heba'i	what happens whenever the
ha-wua mat g kawiyu wo ha-keihi,	horse bucks you off or whenever it kicks,
mat g jiawul wo mumkic.	then the devil makes them sick.
Mañ hab kaij, mo woho matp heg,	What I said, that it's true,
heba'i woi ha-wua,	whenever it bucks them off,
mat heba'i hema kawiyu	whenever a horse
wo t-keihi,	kicks us,
mat heba'i pi huhug g s-ko'ok,	whenever that pain won't go away,
t e-wua mat b o cei,	and what someone will say is,
"Mat o s-ap'e	"It's better to go
wo ñeid g ma:kai."	see a shaman."
T ñeid g ma:kai!	So go see a shaman!
T woho hab wo cei	It's true that he'll say
mat jiawul t-mumkicud,	that the devil is making us sick,
o g haiwañ wo s-ko'okam t-ju:,	or if a cow hurts us,
o g kawiyu p ṣa mo si i	or if a horse bucks us off
t-wua,	accidently,
pi ha'icu wehejiḍ,	just for no reason,
o wo t-ki'iṣ,	or will bite us,
o t-melickwa pi ha'icu wehejiḍ.	or run into us for no reason.
Ṣ e:p jiawul hab ju:,	But the devil caused it,
hekaj t-melickwa.	that's why they run over us.
Hekaj woho mo heg mo	So it's true what is
hega'i t-mumkicud,	making us sick,
jejawul wehejiḍ	from the devils,
kakawiyu ha-amjed,	from the horses,
ha'icu duakam, ha-amjed haiwañ.	and other animals, from cows.
Kakawiyu mat kawiyu abṣ	Horses will just
s-pehegim wua,	automatically buck us off,
o keihi pi ha'icu wehejiḍ,	or kick us for nothing,
o t-ki'iṣ.	or will bite us.

Ṣ hab-a heg wuḍ o	But it is from
mumkidag gḍhu jiawul mat hab	the devil sickness,
wo cei g ma:kai.	the shaman will say.
Ñe, hega'i mat heba'i	Look, at times when something
hema mat g kawiyu	like a horse
m-ki'iṣ mo heba'i,	at times will bite you,
hab e-wua mat abṣ	like they do, and from there
amjedkam abṣ	on it'll just start to
wo m-mumkic,	make you sick, and here the
abṣ o ge'eda hi:wdag,	sore will just grow big,
o g toskoñ,	or the swelling,
o g mat abṣ om ce:dagi.	or the bruise will just turn green.
Mat hema hab wo cei g ma:kai,	When a medicine man says,
"Mat o si e-wuso,	"That you'll get cured,
heba'i gi'ik	at times a four
s-cuhugam mat wo e-wuso,	nights cure,
wo ha'i ha-a:gid,	hire some people,
amhu'i hetasp o gi'ik,	about four or five,
wo e-wusot."	and then they will cure."
O heba'i hema hab e:p cece matk	Or at times one will say to
ṣa:gid e:p losalo	go ahead and also ask
e:p wo ha'i ha-a:g,	someone to run the rosary,
k ho'ige'idahun.	and to be praying.
Hekaj hega'i wuḍ i	So it is from that
hega'i mo heg hab e-wua,	that it will happen,
mat heg wua i hekihu.	that they will cure it.
Heba'i s-woho, c elid g hugid,	At times they [devils] believe, and cure it,
hega'i ha'icu mat s-ko'ok,	that which hurts,
t hega'i hi:wdag.	and heals the sore.
C hega'i ha'icu,	From all of those things,
mat hab o juñim k abṣ	they'll just
o e-wuso mat g	cure it from what the
ma:kai hab o cei.	shaman will say.
Tk wo hekihu hega'i	That will cure all of that
jiwaul mumkidag, jiawul himdag.	devil sickness, devil way.
Ñe, ñt hab e:p abṣ wo cei,	Look, this is what I'll also say,
mac hab kaij,	what we O'odham say,
mo pi-ap hu'i ha-ñeidok,	that they didn't look at their horse the right way,
e-ṣoṣoiga, kakawiyu,	their animals, horses,

c hegam ha'icu,	and other things,
mac heg hab e:p ha-a:g k haiwañ.	and it's what we also say about the cows.
Mo ha'ic mo hab si	Some people just really
ha-cuggia g e-ṣoṣoiga,	fight their horses,
mat heba'i o e-ṣawant mat,	when there is a roundup,
ck haiwañ ha-ñeid,	and they are looking for their cows,
mat heba'i hema am has wo	when someone's horse will do
ṣ a'al e-ju: g e-ṣoiga,	something just a little wrong,
c t-an a'ai wo si-wanckwupad,	and they'll start yanking it back and forth,
c wo 'a'ai si memelicu:dad	and will just run them and
si wanckwupad,	yank them back and forth,
k am o si gewitanad,	and they'll whip it,
c am o si gewitanad,	and will really whip it,
c am o si s-ko'okam has,	and will really hurt it,
oia heg hab ha-mumkicud,	and so that's why it makes them sick,
k hemajkam ha-a'ahed	it reaches those people,
g jiawul mumkidag,	that devil sickness,
c abṣ si ha-kuḍut.	and they really bother them.
Mat k am wo abṣ	People should just be
s-ap ha-cikpanacuḍaḍ,	real careful working with them,
s-ap hab woi ha-ñeidad.	and be nice to them.
Hems hab e-wua	And here they will
c abṣ si ha-kuḍutad,	just really pester them,
ṣ hab-a ama'i pi abṣ	but it's not only on the
cikpan,	job,
c eḍ abṣ cum hekid,	it can be at anytime,
hema am e-ki:kam,	someone at their own home,
o abṣ heba'icuc abṣ	or at times just
inhu abṣ hasko,	anywhere else,
ha'i ha-ṣoṣoiga ha-wehejiḍ,	to someone else's horse,
ha'ap mat hema am	especially if an animal
ha-ki:kam wo jiwa,	comes to somebody's house,
c wo ha-kuḍutad,	and will bother them,
t'b'o gewitan am has wo i wuad,	and they start whipping it and doing something to it,
wo s-ko'okam wuad g ha-ṣoiga,	will be hurting it, someone else's horse,

ok hejel e-ṣoiga
kawiyu wo s-ko'okam wuad.
Wa:m heg hab si e-wua
mat hekiḍ wo ṣa ha-e'eḍ
ab ha-gewitan,
k heg hab si e-wua,
c heg si s-ta-e:bidam,
mat o si s-ko'okam t-mumkic,
wo si s-ko'okam t-a'ahe.

Heba'i wo t-wo'ikuḍ,
pi wo t-himidt,
o pi wo t-ñencud,
mo hab masma ha-a'ahed,
g jiawul mumkidag,
k kawiyu amjed mac
pi-ap hab hu'i ha-ñeidag,
ha'icu i t-ṣoṣoiga,
kakawiyu.
C hab amjed hega'i haiwañ,
hab-a masma e:p hega'i kawiyu,
mo hab-a masma hab e:p cu'igk,
haiwañ, mac hab t-wua,
c heba'i heg hab hi'a e:p e-wua,
mac an ha-kokda piast eḍa,

m-ina pipiast,
mac heba'i pi-ap ha-kokda.

O heg e:p mac an hab kaij,
"Mat heba'i hema pi-ap wo cu'ig,"
t-oksga a:cim pi-ap wo cu'ig,

t-wo a'ahe,

o a'ahe g ali, o a:cim wo t-a'ahe, t-oksga,
heg hab e:p cu'ig e:p,
mat pi-amhu ṣa'i wo ñeidad,
mat hekid wo hema e-mua

or will hurt
his own horse.
That goes especially for
when you make a horse bleed by
whipping them,
and that does particularly,
and that's very dangerous,
that will really make us sick,
or will really give us pain when it reaches us.

Sometimes it will put us in bed,
and will cripple us,
or will blind us,
as it reaches them that way,
the devil sickness,
and from the horse when we're
not careful with them,
all of our animals, like
horses.
And about the cattle,
it's just like the horses,
it will do the same thing,
the cows, like we do,
and at times it also happens,
when we've slaughtered cows for our dances,
for the dances we have,
and at times when we don't kill them the proper way.
Or at times what we say,
"So-and-so isn't perfect,"

or if our wife is "not perfect" [is pregnant],
the sickness will reach us [the parents],
or will reach the baby,

or will reach us or our wife,
and it's also like that,
that they shouldn't watch,

g haiwañ piast eḍ.	whenever they kill
C eḍa e:p mo ṣawant,	a cow for a feast.
c eḍ mat an ha'i e:p	And also during a roundup,
ha-gewpk haiwañ,	and at times
hi abṣ cum ha-ñankogid,	when we pen some cows,
ṣ hab-a s-ko'okam ha-wua,	we just play with them,
c hab-a e:p s-ta-e:bidam	but we accidently hurt them,
hab-a e:p haiwañ cikpan,	and so it's also dangerous
c heg hi abṣ cum	to work and play with cows,
s-ta:hadcud,	and here we are just trying to
c hab ha-wua ṣ hab-a	be happy,
ama s-ko'okam ha-wua,	and in doing that we
t hab-a e:p wuḍ a'ahe hab	accidently injure them,
masma	and that will also reach us
mac hemu an hab e:p kaij	just like
g kawiyu mumkidag,	what we said about
hekaj hab-a masma hab e:p	the horse sickness,
cu'ig g haiwañ,	so that's why it is
wehejiḍ kawiyu	like that cow, horses
c haiwañ mumkidag.	and cows cause devil sickness.

The physical mistreatment of livestock is the definitive *cause* of devil sickness. Thus, the etiology of devil sickness is as follows: A person intentionally or unintentionally mistreats (this can be physical or intellectual mistreatment) or disrespects a cow or horse. At a later, unspecified time, a cow or horse kicks, bites, or throws that person. The person might then have devil sickness and will experience symptoms at some nonspecified time in the future.

Any horse or cow can make a person sick, but it is also not necessary for it to be the same animal that was initially mistreated or disrespected by a person. This is because staying sickness contagion does not connect to the exact animal that causes the sickness, since the sickness does not actually stem from a specific, identifiable, living animal. Instead, contagion derives from the supernatural, spirit "way" of, in this case, the devil, and it is not manifested in a single specific material form.

Devil sickness is perhaps unique in the O'odham theory of sickness. Devils have dominion over horses and cattle. By implication, mistreatment or disrespect toward devils is a transgression against devil property, not against the devil cowboys themselves. No other staying sickness, to our knowledge, operates in exactly this manner. For instance, a transgression against deer way *(huawi himdag)* is a direct transgression against a deer: How is a deer hunted and killed? Is the appropriate prayer offered to the deer? How is it butchered and the meat distributed? The rules of correct handling must be followed; otherwise, deer way is transgressed. Our point is that to transgress against deer way is to transgress not only against deer way, but also a deer. And so is the case for all other spirit ways. Logically, and following from this common etiology, one might expect that a transgression against devils would be some impropriety against devils rather than their possessions (cattle, horses).

There is yet another way of getting devil sickness. Cattle are slaughtered for celebrations of all kinds. This is the ideal use of one's cattle, and of wealth in general, because such use is a public gesture of goodwill toward others. Weddings, saints' feast days, wakes, death anniversaries, and dances are all occasions when cattle are slaughtered to feed guests. To correctly kill a cow means to do so without causing the animal undue terror and pain. The man selected to cut the animal's throat tries to accomplish his task in one quick motion. Failure means that the cow suffers needlessly. Some O'odham say that botching this task is due to a pregnant or menstruating woman who is standing nearby, watching the slaughter. It is thought that her presence adversely affects the ability of the man to carry out his task. As a result, devil sickness may visit the one who killed the cow ineptly, the unborn child of the woman, or even the parents of the unborn child. To avoid future sickness, it is advised that women not watch the slaughter take place.

DL:

Ñe, hega'i a'al,	Look, those babies,
c hegam ha'icu	and those who are
mo ha'ic ge'egeḍ a'al,	adults as well,
haba masma hab e-wua mo	they all catch that
bebbe hega'i jiawul mumkidag,	devil sickness the same way,
no pi ha'i ha-o:g,	because at times their father,
ha-ge'egelid,	or guardian,
mo g s-wapkialim ha'icu cikpan,	who work as cowboys,

t-wenog wo hoñig ha pi-ap cu'ig,	during that time they will not be healthy,
b o e-a'aga cu'igodag,	what we say is pregnancy,
wenog imhu wo	by that time they'll be
cikpan,	working,
k hegam ha-o:g,	and their fathers,
c s-ko'okam ha wua g	and they will hurt the
ha'icu duakam, kakawiyu,	animals, horses,
o g haiwañ,	or cows,
t g wo a'ahe g ali	and it will reach the child
am heba'i ge'edag,	when it begins to grow older,
o mat abṣ al,	or if it's still a baby, when
c mac wo i wu:ṣañ,	it is newborn,
k wo a'al mo hemu hab e-wua,	and right now what kids do,
g wepcij a'al mo	the young people,
s-hohhoid g ṣawant,	while on the roundups,
mat wuid ha abṣ five years	when they'll be about five years
old,	old
s-hohhoid mat wo ha oi g	they like to go out with the
wapkial,	cowboys,
ha-we:m cikpan g ha'icu	and help them work with the
duakam,	animals,
haba e-wua,	and they do this,
c pi e-ñeñeid ha'icu,	and yet they don't watch out
k abṣ am	for themselves, and they just
has juñim eḍa	do anything, and here they
pi s-ma:c hascu	don't understand that it is
s-ta-e:bidam,	dangerous,
c hab-a masma ha-a'hepaḍ,	and how it can reach them,
jiawul mumkidag,	that devil sickness,
hemu g wecij	right now with the young
hemajkam.	people.

"Playing" with cattle can also lead to devil sickness. Cowboys practice chasing and roping the cattle that they have corralled during roundup. It is fun but dangerous play, dangerous because even the most benign play can be too rough for the cattle, and it may lead to the animal's injury. As with horses, the poor treatment of cattle by humans may lead to sickness.

Symptomology

Symptoms distinguish one staying sickness from another, yet symptoms rarely provide the shaman with adequate clues of their patient's condition. As Bahr et al. (1974, 114–16) have discussed, symptoms can be misleading and problematical, and diagnosis elusive. Ultimately, a shaman's ability to see *(ñeid),* to divine the sickness, is necessary for ascertaining precise causality.

The brief diagnosis *(kulañmad)* is used for relatively unproblematical diagnoses, in which a patient's statement of symptoms is largely adequate for a proper diagnosis, or at least for setting the shaman on the right diagnostic track. A more problematic diagnosis requires the longer *duajida* session, when, for instance, several sicknesses are stratified within the patient, or when the stated symptoms form an incomplete picture.[1] Thus, Underhill (1946, 265) was both right and wrong when she stated that symptoms and their disease cause have no relation. She was right in that in some cases, sicknesses have become stratified, and symptoms in this case are not an accurate or complete gauge of an illness event. She was wrong in that symptoms are definitely related to specific sicknesses (Bahr et al. 1974).

The symptoms of devil sickness have been identified in the literature as heart pains caused by a horse hair lodged in the heart and localized pain due to animal bites or kicks (Bahr et al. 1974; Underhill 1946). But there are several other symptoms of this illness such as sleepiness *(ko:sim).* Some have told us that devil sickness makes the sufferer want to "sleep" *(s-ta-ko:simcud).* It is said that this sleep "covers us" *(t-ma'iṣ)* and that it makes people "feel funny" *(ta:hadag).* Dizziness *(noḍagcud)* is yet another symptom and is related to sleepiness. These symptoms are shared with jimsonweed, owls, and peyote sickness and are manifested in a person acting as if he or she is "drunk."

If the symptoms were all that the shaman had to go on for diagnostic purposes, diagnosis would certainly be a much less accurate process. Other cues assist the shaman, including the circumstances that the patient reveals. If the patient is a cowboy and has been bucked off his horse, for example, it is logical that devil sickness rather than, say, jimsonweed sickness is the likely cause. But if someone has had nightmares about deceased relatives, an owl rather than a devil probably caused the sickness.

Fever or heat *(s-toñ)* is also implicated with devil sickness. The status of *s-toñ* in the O'odham theory of sickness is not fully understood. Bahr et al. (1974, 34–36) explain that *s-toñjig* is primarily a manifestation of wandering sicknesses like colds and flus. But they also suggest that a horse's heart is hot, and that this heat can be transferred to a person afflicted with devil sickness. This transfer is articulated as "that fever which reaches us from the devil" *(s-toñjig t-a'ahe ab jiawul t-amjed)*. Both cows and horses have "fever breath," and because cowboy work brings cowboys into close proximity to this dangerous quality, they are likely to experience it as a symptom. Presumably, once a person gets devil sickness, he or she may complain of a fever. Fever breath is contagious not simply for the cowboy, but also for a cowboy's unborn child if his wife is pregnant, his wife, and other relatives. To our knowledge, *s-toñ,* as an aspect of staying sickness, is limited to devil sickness.

Who Is Susceptible?

So far we have emphasized that cowboys, their unborn offspring, and their wives are primarily susceptible to devil sickness. Like other staying sicknesses, devil sickness is not limited by gender, status, or occupation. But it should come as no surprise that cowboys are at the greatest risk of contracting this illness. One could predict that other staying sicknesses also have their more typical victims. For instance, it is likely that deer hunters in the past, men chosen by the elder male of the family, would be most likely to contract deer sickness. Similarly, the warrior who took an Apache scalp (*o:b,* or enemy object) in warfare would be most likely to get sickened by enemy sickness. Owl sickness, on the other hand, is perhaps a more universally contracted staying sickness in that all people have an equal chance of being bothered by the ghost of one's own deceased family members. There are others who are also susceptible to devil sickness.

DL:

Hega'i mo hemu si hekaj,	Those who use horse hair,
mo g u'uwi hekaj	what the ladies use around
eḍa,	here,
k cecoj ha'i hab-a e:p	and some men also use
hekaj kawiyu bahi	the horse tail
huata, mo hemu hab-a	for basketmaking, and now

e:p hekajiḍ cecoj.	the men use it too.
Mo heba'i g wonom giwuḍ na:to,	At times men make hat bands,
c ha'icu mo hekihu	and other things, like
mañ s-ma:c ñ-wosibaḍ,	I know my late grandpa,
mo hab i wua,	that he did,
c heg na:to kawiyu bahi wijina,	and he made horse-tail ropes, and also
c heg e:p si:nju.	cinches.
Ha'ap pi ha-nolot wap	That's why he didn't buy
an g milgan ha-si:nju.	a white-man-made cinch.
Hejel na:to g e-wipijina,	He made his own ropes,
c g he sisi:nju,	and his own cinches,
c hemu mo hab e-wua, g	and right now they use it, the
u'uwi,	ladies,
c g hekaj hua wam hemu	and they are now making horsehair baskets,
mo g e-mu'ij s-ma:c,	and many of them are good,
ck hekaj ha'icu ha-na:to	and they make lots of things
hegam mo ḍ kokomkcuḍ,	like turtles,
o g cu:wi, o g cu:ckuḍ.	or rabbits, or owls.
U'uwi g ha'icu	The shamans say
mo hab ha-a'aga g mamakai	to these ladies
mat hab wo cum ṣa i e-ba:bagi	that they should kind of slow down
hekaj mo s-namkig,	because baskets cost a lot,
am wuḍ ha'icu hega'i, c	they are expensive things, and
mu'i lial, na:to cum ha-a'aga	they make a lot of money, that's why they tell them
mat hab o ṣa i e-ba:bagi,	to try to slow down,
hekaj ha-mumkicud g jejawul.	because the devil is what is making them sick.
Heba'i ha'i ha-nonḍagcud,	Some of them become dizzy,
c e-kukulañmad.	and they go get cured.
Ha'i ab hia si e-ba:bagid,	Some of them do slow down, and
eḍa si keg wuḍ lial,	here it is very good money,
k heg tacu hekaj na:to,	and they need that,
tk s-hohhoid hab e-wua,	and they enjoy doing it,
c ha'ic e-lialga tacu,	and some need the money,
c cum hekid huat na:to	and they are constantly making baskets
heg hekaj kawiyu bahi hua,	from that horse tail,

mo heg s-namkig hemu.
C hekaj s-ta-e:bidam,
hega'i jiawul mumkidag,
kawiyu bahi huata,
mo g hemu s-hohhoid u'uwi
heg hekaj s-huata hega'i.

because they are expensive.
And here it is dangerous,
that devil sickness,
horse-tail basket weaving,
that the ladies enjoy
making baskets with.

5

Devil Songs and the Cure of Devil Sickness

And that's what the devils really like—their songs. And for other spirits that make you sick, they really like to hear their songs, and that will make the patient feel fine.

Song-poetry is the pinnacle, the hallmark, of today's O'odham oral literature. Currently active song genres include social dance *(keihina),* drinking *(i'e),* rain *(nawait i'ita* and *gohimeli),* sickness diagnostic *(duajida),* and curing *(wusot).* The musics are sung by men and women, young and old. Songs are a living, vibrant aspect of native culture. Here we analyze the musics of Wiṣag Woi'i (Hawk Flying) and Jose Manol, who provide poetically compelling and compositionally comparable song-sets.[1] We find song *(ñe'i)* to be a densely meaningful literature, and a literature that speaks to questions of culture history. As literature, both Hawk Flying's and Manol's sets present a structured narrative of dream-journeys whereby the dreamer, the "I" voice in song, is visited by devils who give gifts to the dreaming human. These gifts are sacramental acts in which a devil massages, breathes upon, or teaches songs to the human dreamer. Devil songs are the linguistic record, a literature of culture history, of mystical encounters—devils performing a sacrament for the benefit of living humans. The song-sets of Hawk Flying and Manol, although recorded approximately seventy-five years apart, are strikingly similar in their general characteristics of song subjects, word order, structural form, and lyric content. There is nothing, it seems to us, that poetically and culturally distinguishes Hawk Flying's devil songs from Jose Manol's.[2]

O'odham song poetry belongs to what Herzog (1928) called the dreamt mythic song series tradition. This tradition includes the musics of the riverine Yuman tribes (Cocopa, Maricopa, Mojave, and Yuma), the Great Basin (Shoshone), and others from southern California (Digueño and others), as well as from Mexico (Yaqui). In this poetic tradition, a song is obtained from a dreamed source, from a spirit (or spirits) who sings the song to a dreaming human. Lyric content suggests that a spirit takes the dreaming human on journeys around the O'odham landscape, and in some instances the songs are acquired at, and are even reflective of, points in this journey. Other songs do not suggest a journey but imply a sedentary kind of dream in which the spirit and human remain in one location. In either case, the song is memorized verbatim by the receptive human dreamer, who then sings the song without altering the lyric and melodic structure. Humans never author or compose a *ñe'i.* O'odham songs originate in the land of spirits, not the land of humans. Once a spirit gives a song to a human, like a mockingbird, the human repeats what he has heard. This is not to minimize the role of the songs' human recipients. It is to emphasize that song inspiration is divine, a blessing for humans, and songs are a type of sacred liturgy.

Such song dreaming is the foundation of O'odham shamanism, a poetic form Bahr (n.d.a, 28) calls "shamanic picture poetry." He says that O'odham shamanic songs "commonly feature first person journeys, and the journeys commonly involve light and heat. For example, a shaman may come upon fire at the end of a quest for the cause of sickness" (Bahr n.d.a). O'odham shamanic poetry is a chromatic (Lévi-Strauss 1969) depiction or portrayal of beautiful landscapes and brightly colored natural phenomena.[3] Manol's devil songs fit into this definition of shamanic picture poetry. In Manol's song-set, for example, the I travels to various locations where dazzling mountains (Song 5), sparkling (Song 20), and illumination (Song 35) are experienced and viewed. The extensive use of first-person language, with an additional emphasis on nouns, in O'odham song raise two interpretive problems: first, just who are the I's of each song, and second, what is the I doing, and who or what is doing it to or with them?

We have come to understand the journeys of the I as the first-person experiences of narrators of events that happen to the person during these nocturnal journeys. Through lyric content the listener of songs learns of the I's encounters and experiences in the spirit world. In many of the Manol songs, it is Manol, or perhaps some other dreamer, who is this I. It is not always possible, however, to say whether Manol is the living human I in each or even any of the songs. The song language does not pronounce on this. Asking the singer, "Who is experiencing that?" is the only way to be certain who the I is in a given song. To our knowledge, Bahr did not ask Manol for this information. We suggest that the Manol song-set narrates of a person in the process of gaining shamanic power to cure devil sickness. Moreover, we believe that this narrative telling comprises a structure common among most if not all O'odham curing sets.

Ñe'i is not the only music in O'odham experience. There are several nonshamanic, non-"traditional" genres. *Waila,* commonly called "chicken scratch," is the social dance music of choice. This polka, two-step, and waltz music derives historically from Mexico (*waila* is the O'odham cognate of the Spanish *baile*). As Griffith (1979) describes, the *waila* in the past fifty years has become the primary fiesta music, displacing the traditional round-dance music of the *keihina. Waila* instrumentation includes saxophone, button accordion, bass guitar, drums, and vocals. As music and dance, a *waila* is now performed in conjunction with Christian celebrations. Saint days, weddings, anniversaries, and graduations are all celebrated with this exciting music.

Christian-influenced musics, hymns, are also popular. Spanish hymns have been part of O'odham religious life for over a century. Adelaide Bahr (n.d.) has noted some similarities between traditional O'odham music and Spanish hymns. Commonalities are found in the structure and repetition patterns, memorization, and the indianization of hymn texts. English hymns have also made their way into O'odham culture. This has occurred since the turn of the century, when Protestant missionaries translated some hymns into O'odham (Haefer 1981, 139). Other adaptations continue to occur. In Santa Rosa, for instance, one performance group sings their own stylized versions of popular rock tunes in the Catholic church to the accompaniment of acoustic and bass guitars.

Rock and roll and country western are both music genres with wide appeal. Teenagers and young adults listen to radio stations and buy tapes of their favorite top-ten recording stars.

Traditional song-poetry is completely different from these other musical styles. Traditional music derives from the spirit world, whereas the other styles come from this-worldly sources. Traditional music has a mythical pedigree, while the other styles do not.

Medicine Songs

There are two classes of O'odham medicine songs: diagnostic and curative. Diagnostic *(duajida)* songs are the exclusive domain of shamans *(mamakai)*. Diagnostic songs are sung during the diagnosis of a sickness or sicknesses. Curative medicine songs can be learned and sung by anyone. They are sung during a curing session called a *wusota,* and when a shaman is not required to attend. Singers of curing songs are called blower people, or ritual curers *(s-wusos o'odham).*

DL:	
Ñe, hega'i m a:cim a:g	Look, that what we say
has mas wuḍ ab	about the
wusosig kc duajida,	curing and diagnosis songs,
mo gawul cu'ig,	that they are different,
cu'ig no pi hega'i wusosig,	because as with the curing,
mat abṣ cumheda'i s-ap	just anyone can
hab o ju:, g hemajkam.	do that, the people.
Cum has pi wuḍ wo ma:kai kc hab,	Even if they aren't a shaman,
ṣ hab-a wo s-ma:c idam ñeñe'i,	people will know the songs,
jiawul ñe'i, c cukuḍ ñeñe'i,	devil songs, and owl songs,
ha'icu i wusosig ñeñe'i.	and other curing songs.
Abṣ cum heda'i s-ap	Just about anyone can
wo wuso g o'odham,	cure people,
cum hema taṣkaj taṣ'eḍ	anytime day
o cuhug,	or night,
abṣ cum he'ekia o:la.	or any hour.
Ab o ha'ic hab e'lidc mo hab	Some people will plan for what
cece g ma:kai mat wo si e-wuso.	the shaman says about how to really cure someone.
Cuhugam oidam e-wusot o maḍ	Like an all-night cure from
huḍuñig amjed wo i ṣon wua	the evening when one begins
g hema cukuḍ wusosig,	with the owl cure,
eḍa hegam s-cuhugam hegam	up to midnight, and the
jejawul wusosig ab haha	devil curing will begin
e:p wo i oi e:p	and go
gmhu wo ma:sig.	until the morning.
K heba'i ha'ic si wusot.	And this will cure a person.
Cehani ha-a'agiḍ heba'i go:k	They tell you to hire two
o waik o gi'ik ñe'ñedkam—	or three or four singers—
hekaj si wusot.	that's when it really cures.

C hega'i duajida mo hab cu'ig,	The diagnosis is something
mo hega'i ma:kai hab i si ap	only the shaman can do
matog hio dahiwa cuhugam oidam.	by sitting during the night.
Heg oidam ha'icu wo mamce,	He will also check other things,
mo ha-kulañmad kc ha-duajida.	medicating and diagnosing.
Mo g ṣawikuḍ hekaj	They use a rattle and a
a'an	feather
ñeid g mumkidag,	to see the sickness,
c ki:dag.	and around the house.
C hekaj ṣa gawul cu'ig,	That's why it's different,
hega'i wusosig c duajida,	curing and diagnosing,
c hega'i ma:kai at-p ap'i si ap,	and it's up to the shaman
hega'i duajida.	to diagnose.
Mat k hio g hio mamce	He'll examine the living area
ki:dag,	and house,
mumkidag, has mas hascu	the sickness, to see
am has cu'ig,	what is around,
hascu mumkicud g hemajkam.	what is making the person ill.
Ha'icu amo wo i e-cu:g,	Something will appear,
hascu wo	whatever he [the shaman] will
pikcul,	picture,
hekaj heg ṣa gawul masma hab	so this is different,
cu'ig wusosig c duajida.	curing and diagnosis.

The two classes of medicine song are distinguished largely by who has access to and who sings them. Curing songs *(wusosig ñeñei)* are sung by anyone who knows *(s-ma:cig)* the appropriate songs for a shaman-diagnosed sickness. *Wuso,* literally, to blow on an object, can be performed by virtually anyone. Despite this democratic approach to curing, a *ma:kai* is thought to accomplish it best. The curing session for devil sickness, as for all staying sicknesses, begins in the evening around sunset *(huḍuñig)* and ideally goes until morning *(ma:sig).* As the Manol set demonstrates, both literal and metaphorical illumination is made at the end of the set. It is in the morning that a cure is completed, hopefully a success. It is at sunrise that things are literally illuminated by sunlight, and metaphorically through the allusions created in the song-set.

Diagnosis songs *(duajida ñeñei)* are the domain of the shaman. Often during a diagnosis the shaman examines not only the patient's body but also where the person lives *(ki:dag)*. In both examinations sorcery objects are sought out and destroyed. Here the shaman uses special tools *(iagta)* for the divination of disease. These tools include rattles *(ṣawikuḍ)*, feathers *(a'an)*, crystals *(tondam hodai)*, and cigarette smoke *(je:ñ)*. These tools enhance or augment the shaman's ability to see *(ñeid)* the sickness-causing entity that permeates the patient's body and home. The shaman is successful when this entity appears *(e-cu:g)* as a vision to him. He pictures *(pikcul)* what is causing the sickness. After diagnosis the patient must then hire singers who know the appropriate curing songs, which the shaman prescribes for the patient's ultimate cure.

In the O'odham theory of sickness, medicine songs are context dependent. That is, it is not the lyric content or the compositional elements of a song that informs the hearer that a song is a diagnostic or a curing song. Rather, it is the context in which songs are sung that define them as diagnostic or curative. It may even be true that a song does not have a final or permanent disposition. Conceivably, it can pull double duty, used in various contexts for various purposes. Does this mean that there are no intrinsic structural or lyrical differences between medicine songs? Lopez claims that Manol's songs could be used in either a diagnostic or curative context. This coincides with Bahr's (1991b, 8–9) analysis of two owl songs of the O'odham shaman John Lewis. According to Bahr, the only, if minor, apparent difference is that an I in *duajida* songs always refers to the *ma:kai,* while an I in *wusosig* songs may possess other referents, human and otherwise.

Hawk Flying's (Demon) Songs

DL:

Hega'i jiawul ñeñe'i	The devil songs
hab am amjed hihim	come from
idam ha'icu duakam,	these different animals,
jejawul inhab i cucu'ig do'ag,	devils around the mountain,
ok ha'icu duakam mo ani	or from other animals that
ha'icuk g jejawul.	are around the devils.
Hegam jejawul	Those devil
ñeñe'i mo heg hekaj	songs that they now use
e-wusot g hemajkam hemu,	to cure the people,
c ha'icu i haiwañ, kakawiyu,	and those from cows, horses,

cu:ckuḍ—mo ḍ	owls—those that are also
wes hegam ha'icu jejawul—	some things like devils—
mo hekid amjed hihim hega'i	that are in
jejawul ñeñe'i,	devil songs,
s-idam do'ag m-in	from the mountains that are
ke:k,	standing around,
matp g hemajkam ha-wui e-cecegid	they appear to people
ha-ce:cka-d hab-a masma i	in their dreams and also
e-cecegid ha'ic ha-u'u ha-	in their songs
ñeñe'i.	at times.
C hekaj e-wusot,	They then use them to cure,
c haba ab ha'ic g hemajkam	and some people
mat hekaj wo ha-wuso wo mai	who are cured from them
ñeñe'i g eḍ a'aga,	say that it is in the songs,
c hekaj wo ha-wuso,	and that's why songs cure,
t wo ha-doa hemajkam.	and get the people well.
Hab amjed hihim hegam	That's where those
jejawul ñeñei,	devil songs come from,
idam ha-amjed ha'icu duakam,	from some kinds of animals,
c do'ag mo g cu:ckuḍ an i	and from the mountains that
wuhak g cuhug.	the spirits emerge from at night.

We begin our analysis of devil songs with a four-song set sung by Hawk Flying as published in Russell (1908). Because we feel that it is crucial for our literary analysis to compare Hawk Flying's songs with Jose Manol's, it is first necessary to do three things with Russell's renditions of Hawk Flying's songs. First, Russell's linguistic format and line assignments in the songs are inaccurate. Russell wrote the songs phonetically and for some reason rendered them in an arbitrarily punctuated (periods, commas, semicolons) paragraph form. Our first task, then, was to rework and repunctuate the songs into lines that would come closer to the original sung forms. Second, we provide ordinary O'odham language translations of the words that Russell wrote only in "song language." There is substantial variation between Russell's and our subsequent reformulation. Providing a revised English version was the third task. The revised versions reflect our revised line divisions, punctuation, and so on.

Each song is presented in each of the three versions: Russell's English, retranslated O'odham, and new English versions.

Song 1
Singing at Ka'matuk mountain
Singing at Ka'matuk mountain
I listen to their singing
I come running to sing with them.

• • •

Komalk do'ag wawañig mu'i ñeñe'i kaiham
Broad mountain lined along many songs listen

Komalk do'ag wawañig mu'i ñeñe'i kaiham
Broad mountain lined along many songs listen

Kuñ am i mel
I came running

I:ya kai m-eḍa ṣaṣawk
Here heard you-inside echo

• • •

AT THE BASE OF BROAD MOUNTAIN I LISTEN TO MANY SONGS
AT THE BASE OF BROAD MOUNTAIN I LISTEN TO MANY SONGS
I COME RUNNING
TO LISTEN TO THE ECHOES

Song 2
Evening now is falling
Evening now is falling
And demons appeared running
To strip and expose my soul.

• • •

Huḍuñig mia ṣoṣonwa
Evening close starting

Huḍuñig mia ṣoṣonwa
Evening close starting

K eḍa g ñeñawul ñe'iopa i:ya wo:po'o
And from inside the devils rush out here running

Ñ-i:bhena dagiomun
Me-breathed massaged

• • •

EVENING CLOSE, IT IS FALLING
EVENING CLOSE, IT IS FALLING
FROM INSIDE, THE DEVILS COME RUSHING OUT
THEY BREATHED ON AND MASSAGED ME

Song 3
In a Santa Rita Cave
In a Santa Rita Cave
As I entered in the cave
I saw the breath of demons.

• • •

Jewa do'ag waŋe m-eḍa ñeñe'i kai
Rotten mountain I entered inside songs sound

Jewa do'ag waŋe m-eḍa ñeñe'i kai
Rotten mountain I entered inside songs sound

G eḍa ñ-ñe'i kai
And inside I songs heard

Kuñdañ-i wa:k ñeid
Inside I entered saw

Kuñda g ñeñawul a'ai mo'o hiwa
There I the devils back and forth heading rubbing

• • •

I ENTERED ROTTEN MOUNTAIN AND HEARD THE SOUNDS OF SONGS
I ENTERED ROTTEN MOUNTAIN AND HEARD THE SOUNDS OF SONGS
AND INSIDE I LISTENED TO THE SONGS
AND INSIDE I SAW
THERE I SAW THE DEVILS ROCKING THEIR HEADS RUBBING

Song 4
Here demon boys come running
Here demon boys come running
Grasping my hair they carried me
Brought me to a distant land.

• • •

Ñeñawul a'ali i:ya wo:po'o
Devil kids here come running

Hiosig ñ-ṣagiḍ ke:k wa
Flowers I between standing

Gmhu me:kjeḍ kawk jeweḍ hekid 'an ñ-i:ya wawpañ
Way far hard land edge [of] me-here stretches

Ñ-i:bhena ñ-i:yai:buiwa
My breath I herepant

• • •

DEVIL KIDS COME RUNNING
I STAND BETWEEN FLOWERS
AND THE DISTANT HARD LAND'S EDGE STRETCHES BEFORE ME
MY BREATH, HERE I PANT

The four songs comprise a poetically unified or inclusive short set of music. This means that the corpus of music tells an unfolding or emergent story, each song akin to the chapter of a book or the act in a play. Individual songs contribute to the set as a meaningful whole. Each song takes life and becomes meaningful once it is placed in a sequence. By implication single songs loose their significance once they are removed from a song-set's overall structure and context.

The significance and importance of sequence in the creation of meaning in music was observed by Lévi-Strauss (1969), and he made the further interesting comparison that exists between music and myth. In both myth and music (he refers to symphonic music), there is a beginning and an end, and in between is a sequencing that evokes both individually felt and collectively held emotions and intellectual responses. He goes so far as to say that the themes and variations of music can only be comprehended and appreciated if the listener keeps the previous themes and variations in mind. What comes before in a piece of music or a myth telling, therefore, is indispensable for understanding the message of either. He argues that "there is a kind of continuous reconstruction taking place in the mind of the listener to music or the listener to a mythic story" (Lévi-Strauss 1995 [1978], 49). For him, the unfolding messages embedded in music and myth follow structural principles of presentation predicated on a universal pattern.

The unfolding character in the structural principle of sequencing is of central theoretical importance in O'odham song-poetry. In fact, the collaborative work of Bahr et al. (1979) establishes the analytic necessity of studying O'odham song-sets rather than isolated songs. They state: "Our thesis on song as literature is that, among Pimans, song becomes a powerful literary form through the use of multi-song sets" (Bahr et al. 1979, 245). Through the analysis of Hawk Flying's set, we demonstrate how this thesis is correct even for this very short set of music.

Beyond the sequencing principle, we hypothesize that all O'odham curing song-sets are structured according to the presentation and resolution of what we call a "primary poetic tension" and a "secondary poetic tension." The primary poetic tension establishes who the "I" and "you" or "they" are in the set. It establishes the song-set's characters for the audience, both human and spirit (recall that curing songs are intended to be heard primarily by the spirit that causes illness). The primary poetic tension corresponds to Lévi-Strauss's generalized contention and to Bahr et al.'s specific thesis, stated above. The secondary poetic tension proposes a philosophic issue, quandary, puzzlement, meditation, or question that demands the listener to contemplate and perhaps resolve (if resolution is called for). For the human audience the secondary poetic tension requests an emotional response and asks that humans empathize with the predicament faced by the song-set's characters to comprehend and resolve the issue or question for themselves. We do not and cannot know what this secondary tension might mean for spirits. Our suspicion is, theoretically at least, that in addition to getting spirits to enjoy hearing their songs—the stated reason among O'odham for why the spirit releases the sick person—a curing set also attempts to get the spirit audience to empathize with the humbleness and prayerfulness implicit in the set.

A set's artistic achievements, in our way of thinking, rely on this secondary poetic tension and its resolution. A successful song-set rests partly on the meanings, symbols, allegories, and emotive and intellectual responses that it elicits from those who hear and attempt to interpret it. In other words, the secrets that can be understood of what a set has to offer are central in medical efficacy.

Each of the four songs possesses first-person language. There is an I or "me" that has an experience. We suggest that this I is, at least rhetorically, the same individual throughout the set and is a living human dreamer (in this case, Hawk Flying). The I is in many ways herolike for being exposed to and receptive of the tutoring provided by devil spirits. Songs 1 and 2 also possess second- and third-person referents. In both cases the "you" and the "they" refer to whom or what confronts the I of the songs. Song 1 establishes the primary poetic tension by raising this question: who is the I that listens to the you? The first song does not offer an answer. It merely raises the question that rhetorically heightens the listener's sense of the dramatic. The song does offer other relevant information. The I is near the Broad Mountains, southwest of

Phoenix, and the I is listening to songs that emanate (and echo) from or near it. The reference to this mountain range is significant in establishing who the "you" is because, according to Russell (1908, 255), "evil spirits [devils] dwell" there. Since devils live in and around mountains, it is safe to assume that the singing emanating from the Broad Mountains in these songs comes from devils. The word echo (*ṣaṣawk*, literally, the place of an echo) is multifaceted and difficult to translate. On the one hand, a literal translation of this word refers to the song's subject, who overhears the song that originates from a spirit source, the place of an echo, and in this case it is a devil mountain. On the other hand, "echo" is a reference to, as Lopez would argue, how songs move around and meet people. It has a mystical and ephemeral quality that is characteristic of "sound." Therefore, *ṣaṣawk* refers simultaneously to place and sound. Our point is that sound, in this case the tonality and perhaps the rhythm of music, is inseparable from the landscape of the song's literary narrative. The importance of sound, it seems to us, is at least equal to the picture-poetic component of O'odham dreaming and song-poetry.

Song 2 answers the primary poetic tension. It informs the hearer that, in the evening, devils emerge from their home and bestow power on the I: "THEY BREATHED ON AND MASSAGED ME." These sacramental acts, according to the O'odham medical system, tutor and endow the living human I with the ability to use the very same techniques in diagnostic sessions or ritual cures: spirits breathe on curers, curers breathe on patients, patients are healed with the sacrament of breath. This song establishes the shamanic credentials of this song-set. This song, and others like it, authenticates or bolsters the singer's claim to medical efficacy. As an M.D. bolsters authority through various devices (diploma, specialized language use, technology), so too the O'odham curers employ devices to reassure their patients.

Song 3 continues the narrative sequencing by telling us what the I experiences while going inside of the devil's home, presumably to learn more. In this case, though the references are vague at best, the I is shown how to use a notched percussion instrument. The critical line says, "THERE I SAW THE DEVILS ROCKING THEIR HEADS RUBBING." The final word of the final line of this song—*hiwa*—literally means "to rub." This word in this song is a cryptically poetic way to say *hiwculid*, "to rub a notched instrument." This notched instrument is used primarily for ritual cures. The first part of this line, "ROCKING THEIR HEADS," refers to the sight of the devils keeping time with the music. Combined, Songs 2 and 3 tell of power acquisition, of a human being tutored by devil spirits.

Song 4, abrupt and challenging, even apocalyptic, closes this short set. This song establishes the secondary poetic tension by creating a strong and intriguing visual image that asks the listener to resolve. The I, after his encounter with devils, arrives at a boundary of sorts. From where the I stands—"BETWEEN FLOWERS," looking toward a "DISTANT HARD LAND"—we sense a moment of hesitation, of movement ceased, while the I states, "MY BREATH, HERE I PANT." We suggest that a key to understanding the shamanic picture poetry of this set, to understanding the secondary poetic tension, lies in answering what this hesitation refers to. We believe that the I is in an existential quandary of sorts between remaining with the devils, where learning has occurred in the seductive flower world (what Lopez calls the "shadow of death"), and where the I could learn more, or returning to the "HARD LAND" (a hot and parched land of the living, and perhaps of mundane existence). We believe it is an apocalyptic choice of life or death. It is apocalyptic because the boundary between the flower world and the hard land is so clear to the I that this boundary is permeable, and life and death are closer than one normally imagines to be true.

The I's panting is also intriguing. Panting may refer in this song to the I of "I COME RUNNING" in Song 1, of being escorted by devils from place to place, of anxiety, or of the shamanic act of the healing breath *(i:bhena)*. The boundary the dreaming human arrives at is one where they are abandoned by the devils. The I's final decision remains lyrically unstated. This implies one of two possibilities: these four songs were part of a larger compilation of music, a long set, that was not recorded by Russell or simply not included in his book; or the audience of this set must decide the significance or efficacy of the secondary poetic tension. In other words, the listeners must decide for themselves the significance of this hesitation. In either case, we are confident that further songs would have added more clues to help the listener solve this existential riddle.

Hawk Flying's songs show us that, taken individually, songs are like snapshots that record a picture of some landscape scene that variously includes mountains, animals, humans, and spirits, a picture of some activity, including references to sight, sound, touch, and movement. Considered as a sequenced set, they present us with an unfolding record of a journey taken by an I.

Song-sets present the audience with two poetic tensions that shed light on the dynamic and phantasmic interaction of spirits and humans. These poetic tensions ask the attentive listener to empathize with the textually generated images and tensions so that an empathetic and vicarious comparison is made between the sick, the healer, and the spirit cause of illness. Consequently, several correspondences can be made. There is an implicit relation between spirit and human, mentor and student, teacher and learner, and singer and patient (audience). Curing songs bridge the boundaries between them by making a phantasmic experience accessible to all.

Jose Manol's Devil Songs

The ritual curer Jose Manol sang the following long set of thirty-five songs in 1977, recorded in Manol's home by anthropologist Donald Bahr.[4] Like the previous short set, this set is for the cure of *jiawul mumkidag*. The songs were sung at Bahr's request and were not recorded during an actual curing session.

The set forms a poetry that offers further insights into the world of devils, the O'odham's shamanistic theory of sickness and cure, and culture history. The question arises as to the extent to which these songs provide evidence for the critique of capitalist-induced culture change. Unlike stories about devils, we find no linguistic evidence that devil songs serve as an indigenous critique or form of resistance. While devils and corollary subjects permeate the songs, song narratives are more about power acquisition of an individual, dreaming human. They are about personal empowerment, not resistance.

Hawk Flying's short set could have been, and perhaps was, used in the cure of devil sickness, but Russell did not provide any documentation on the songs' significance or use. Manol's set provides a compelling account of the use of O'odham epic song-poetry for the maximal cure of devil sickness, and of a set that was used in cures of devil sickness.[5]

Performance questions arise in analyzing the Manol set. Is it appropriate to make generalizations about curing from a song-set that was performed outside of a curing context? Does performance context effect a song-set's meaning? Whereas a performance recording would be ideal, we do not think there is a problem in analyzing the textual song-set offered here. The proof of their comparability and shared meaning lies in the structure of the song-set. Overall song sequence is fixed by the singer. In this case Manol fixed the devil songs into an assemblage unique to his creative sensibility. Spirits compose songs, but they do not arrange them into sets. While Manol may not have dreamt all the of the songs himself, he did arrange these thirty-five songs into the set presented below. Bahr et al. (1979, 251) says, "Singers normally fix their repertoire for a given type of song so as to sing the same songs in the same sequence whenever that type of song is called for." This means that a song-set will be sung in the established sequence whether in a cure or under the unusual circumstance of a private music lesson for an anthropologist.

One may legitimately ask: could the song-set sequence have been altered by Manol? The answer is yes, although it is unlikely. When a singer fixes his repertoire, he does so to tell a narrative using numerous individual songs. It is perhaps a process not so different from that of a historian who tells a history using numerous documentary sources. With this said, we must report that Manol's devil-song set was recorded only once, by Bahr, during a private music lesson. We have no conclusive way to compare this recorded set with that of an actual curing session. Consequently, we cannot be absolutely certain if Manol altered the sequence of the songs in this set. Our impression is that he did not. First, altering a set of this size would be immensely difficult and confusing for the singer. It takes tremendous effort and creativity to memorize a long set. A set's sequence is fixed in memory to recall it—in sequence—when needed. It seems to us that intentionally scrambling the sequence would prove tremendously difficult and a frankly improbable maneuver. Second, mixing up the sequence amounts to garbling the singer's story, the moral of the message, obscuring its intended poetic tensions and intentions and creative structure. Third, we can "verify" the set's structural integrity by analyzing how the set "fits" together. We may ask of the set: Do the songs tell a progressively unfolding story? Does the song order make sense? Is the narrative coherent? Are there well-developed primary and secondary poetic tensions? Our answer is yes to each of the above questions, and we believe that Manol's devil songs were probably sung in the same sequence in a cure as they are presented here.

Our method of answering these questions, as detailed in chapter 1, followed four steps. To briefly reiterate those steps: First, we aligned song beats with word syllables. This step fixes the song language in how it is actually sung in O'odham in the syllabic and metrical form. Second, we obtained a literal O'odham translation that was derived exclusively from the sung form of the previous step. Third, we obtained a free O'odham translation, a step not reproduced in this book. Fourth, we made a free English translation that attempts to stay as close as possible to the original O'odham linguistic and poetic style. Lopez offers an interpretation/critique of each song text.

Jejawul Ñeñe'i[6]

Song 1

1.													
Ta		ṣawa		hu	ne	ñi	ma						
2.													
Ke		taŋ	ge	ñe	ña	wu	li	ah		ali			
ñei	opa	ke	wo	po	hi	ma							
3.													
Ña	na	ko		ko	ŋa	hio	ho	sime	ia				
pa	ñe	cuŋi	ok										
4.													
Ka		wañi	woho	woi	wawo		poi	mam					

1. Taṣ huḍuñig
2. Kt aigo ñeñawul a'al ñe'iopa wo:po
3. Ñ kugiwa hiosig pañe ce:k
4. K wa ñ-wui wo:po

1. FROM WHERE THE SUN SETS
2. THE DEVIL KIDS APPEARED
3. THEY COVER ME IN FLOWER PETALS
4. AS THEY RUN PAST

That person in the song went west in a dream; that's when he got the song. Devil kids came to him from the west to meet him [Jose]. That's where the devil kids live. They put flowers on him, rubbed him with flowers. I have never heard of devils doing this because they usually use horse hair, not flowers. But I suppose that it's the same thing. That's what it means when I have said that other places, villages, have their own ways of dreaming. Other places do things a little bit differently.

Song 2

| | | | | | | | | | | | |

1.
Hunu ñisi mia mo ña ma ci bu no cu'i
ñano si hi ku li
2.
Hunu ñisi mia mo ña ma ci bu no cu'i
ñamo si hi ku li
3.
Gamo mulk go cu kañi ina ṣu taŋi ku mui
taŋi ju mali ge sima geda wa kime

| | | | | | | | | | | | |

1. Huḍuñig s-mia mo ñ-ma:c pi-cu'ig ñ-si'ihegi
2. Huḍuñig s-mia mo ñ-ma:c pi-cu'ig ñ-si'ihegi
3. Gamhu ñ ṣudagi ku:gitahim jumal gesi eḍa wa:k

1. THE EVENING IS NEAR, DON'T KNOW WHAT HAPPENED TO MY ELDER BROTHER
2. THE EVENING IS NEAR, DON'T KNOW WHAT HAPPENED TO MY ELDER BROTHER
3. FAR AWAY AT THE WATER'S EDGE, I ENTERED INSIDE

I don't know if this song is talking about the ocean or the Colorado River, or if it's around here somewhere. The song doesn't say. This is kind of funny and I am not really sure what it means. But devils do live in the water too, not just in some mountains. I don't know why this song is in here. I think that the older brother refers to the dreamer's brother, not I'itoi. The brother must have died or something.

Song 3

| | | | | | | | | | | | |

1.
Hunu ñisi mia mo ña me ṣo ṣo na
2.
Hunu ñisi mia mo ña me ṣo ṣo na
3.
Gena tañe ña wu li ñei opa kai
4.
I ya we wui wa ba ñi boi ta ge
taŋo ma hima

| | | | | | | | | | | | |

1 Huḍuñig s-mia ñe'i ṣo:ṣon
2. Huḍuñig s-mia ñe'i ṣo:ṣon
3. G eḍa ñeñawul ñe'iopa
4. I:ya wa wui i:bheni eḍa dagimuna

1. WITH THE EVENING CLOSE THE SONGS BEGIN
2. WITH THE EVENING CLOSE THE SONGS BEGIN
3. FROM INSIDE THE DEVILS EMERGED
4. WHERE THEY BREATHED ON ME, AND MASSAGED ME

The devils came to Jose and breathed on and massaged him; that means that they gave him power to cure other people. The devils did to Jose what a medicine man does to his patients. The massaging and breath teaches Jose how to cure properly. Devils and other spirits are like tutors.

Song 4

1.												
Hu	ḍuñi	mi		mia	ge	ñe	ña	wu	li	ñei	opa	
2.												
Hu	ḍuñi	mi		mia		ge	ñe	ña	wu	li	ñei	opa
3.												
Sapo	kai		ta	mo	ñei	kai	cu	kaŋi				
ka	cime	wesi	koio	ŋi	hi	me						

1. Huḍuñig mia g ñeñawul ñe'iopa
2. Huḍañig mia g ñeñawul ñe'iopa
3. S-ap'e kaidag m-ñe'i kaid c ku:g ka:cim wesko ku:gi

1. THE DEVILS APPEARED AS DARKNESS APPROACHED
2. THE DEVILS APPEARED AS DARKNESS APPROACHED
3. THEIR SONGS SOUND BEAUTIFUL AS EVENING FALLS OVER THE EDGE

Night is close by. The sun is falling over the edge of the land; you know, the sun goes down. That's when the devils come out; they wake up and are awake all night long. The person, the I, is standing and looking toward the night and sees the devils come out.

Song 5

1.												
Si		wo	da	to	no	we	ga	mu	na	cu		
ñe	kai		me									
2.												
Si		wo	da	to	no	we	ga	mu	na	cu		
ñe	kai		me									
3.												
Muna	cu	ñe	kai		him							
4.												
Ku	na	ñi	wawa		ko	ñei		ta				
5.												
Ku	na	ga	ñe	ña	wul		ah	ai	mo	hai	wa	

1. Si:woda dodoag m-eḍa c ñ-kai
2. Si:woda dodoag m-eḍa c ñ-kai
3. M-eḍa ñ-kaiham
4. Eḍa ñ-wa:k k ñeid
5. Eḍa g ñeñawul a'ai mo'o wa

1. INSIDE THE DAZZLING MOUNTAIN I LISTENED
2. INSIDE THE DAZZLING MOUNTAIN I LISTENED
3. INSIDE I HEARD
4. AND I WENT INSIDE AND SAW
5. THE DEVILS SHAKE THEIR HEADS

This song is a hard one to catch. This mountain is shining; and inside the devils are singing. Jose goes in and sees them sitting there singing. The devils are happy to see him, and show him that they are happy because they are rocking their heads back and forth; they're dancing with their head. Maybe they're singing, but the song doesn't say that they are. The King devil is like a roundup boss. He's called u:gcu'u *in Papago.*

Song 6

1.												
Cu		wai	we	to	no	waŋa	ke	nama	to	ñe	ñei	
ñe	wa	ka	kana	ki	ma							
2.												
Koñ	ali	ka	kai	yoka	wo		whoi	mo	ḍai	hi	ñima	

3.
Woi wiŋi ke ki wa ke we siko ñ ta ŋo
4.
Kuña hu na wi piyo si ma
| | | | | | | | | | | | |

1. Cecu do'ag eḍa ñeñe'i ñ-wa:ki kime
2. Kuñ al kai k wui oi mo ḍahi
3. Wui ñ-ke:kad wesko ñ-dagimuna
4. Kuñ eḍa wipiot

1. THE SONGS MAKE ME ENTER LONG MOUNTAIN
2. I MOVED CLOSER AS I LISTENED
3. HE STOOD NEAR AND MASSAGED ME
4. AND THREW HIS STRENGTH INSIDE ME

This one's kind of hard too. Jose went into the mountain where the devils are; they are singing their songs. He was really showing interest in what they were singing. He sat close and leaned forward to catch it. Maybe the devil liked him and told Jose to open his mouth. The devil threw up into him, wipiot *we say, and gave him a song. That went into his mind so that it would help him to remember the song. It goes into your mind so you won't forget; it's in your imagination.*

Song 7
| | | | | | | | | | | | |
1.
Wa to si ju kime ki na na ko
kai ci ta na
2.
Wa to si ju kime ki na na ko
kai ci ta na
3.
Ah ci oi daŋe gaŋa koli ṣu ṣu gai
4.
Ñe wa ño si ñei damo gia hime huna
| | | | | | | | | | | | |

1. Wa si ju:ki si na:nko kaij
2. Wa si ju:ki si na:nko kaij
3. Achi oidak eḍa ali ṣu:dagi
4. Ñ wa ñ si ñeid mo gahi him

1. THERE ARE MANY DIFFERENT SOUNDS WHEN IT RAINS
2. THERE ARE MANY DIFFERENT SOUNDS WHEN IT RAINS
3. AND WATER STANDS IN ACHI FIELDS
4. I ADMIRE THEM AS I WALK

I think this happened in the daytime, not at night. It was raining and thundering. Jose was listening to all the sounds, and he got the song. He was walking around his fields near Gu Achi. There were little ponds of water standing around over there.

Song 8

| | | | | | | | | | | | |

1\.
Wa ṣal si si ko li ṣu ṣu ki ma
2\.
Wa ṣal si si ko li ṣu ṣu ki ma
3\.
Oita koi ñabai cu hi ma
4\.
Ge hi na ge ñe ña wuli ah ha li ñe he
ñe we kai naŋ

| | | | | | | | | | | | |

1. Wa al sikol ṣu:dagi
2. Wa al sikol ṣu:dagi
3. Oida ñ-behima
4. G hiwigid ñeñawul a'al ñe'i ñ-kai

1. SWIRLING WATER
2. SWIRLING WATER
3. ALONG THERE THEY LEAD ME
4. THE DEVIL KIDS SING TO ME THEIR SONGS

The devil kids gave him this song in his sleep. They showed him around the water. Jose follows the devil kids around to different places. This happened in his dreams.

Song 9

| | | | | | | | | | | | |

1\.
Ñia wu li on na me ba ma toi ñai
be hi cu kai ma
2\.
cu ka ki taŋo ma ge kona koi ñe wañe me huna

| | | | | | | | | | | | |

1. Ñiawul o'odham heba'i ñ-behe
2. Cuhugam g ñ-wañimed

1. DEVIL PEOPLE WHERE ARE YOU TAKING ME?
2. ALONG THE DARKNESS YOU LEAD ME

The devils appear to him in the middle of the night; they're walking. He follows them. The song is talking about the night. The devils are taking him somewhere, maybe to their devil mountain, their home.

Song 10

| | | | | | | | | | | | |

1.
Ñe ña wu li ia ŋa ta me he ḍawa
ko ko gai ma
2.
Ñe ña wu li ia ŋa ta me he ḍawa
ko ko gai ma
3.
Wa ñoi si bama ña moi da hi ma
4.
Cu ka kai oi na ga me hu da wa
ko hu ko gai mam

| | | | | | | | | | | | |

1. Ñeñawul iagta mehe eḍa ku:gidahim
2. Ñeñawul iagta mehe eḍa ku:gidahim
3. Wa ñ-oi si behe oidahim
4. Cuhug oid gamhu heba'i ku:gidahim

1. INSIDE ARE THE DEVIL'S TOOLS
2. INSIDE ARE THE DEVIL'S TOOLS
3. I WENT AHEAD AND FOLLOWED
4. AT NIGHT I FOLLOWED TO WHERE THEY END

This song uses a hard word. I kind of didn't catch it at first, but I got it. That word, iagta, *it means something like devil's things, medicine man things, the devil's tools. You know, like a feather or rock, a crystal, the things that a shaman uses. I don't really get "where they end." But Jose followed them.*

Song 11

| | | | | | | | | | | | |

1.
Kaña ge ñi ha wu li

2.
Kaña ge ñi ha wu li
3.
Si nuña tat ha ma no li lia ta no
ko ko kai ma li
4.
Oi ka pame li oi ka pime li juñ am
| | | | | | | | | | | | |

1. K ñ-g ñiawul
2. K ñ-g ñiawul
3. I:ya ñ-da:m liliat ku:gidahim
4. I:da mel oik ap i mel juñim

1. I'M A GREAT DEVIL
2. I'M A GREAT DEVIL
3. ABOVE ME THE LARIAT SWINGS
4. GO AHEAD AND SWING IT

The devil shows the person how to use a rope and tells him to go ahead and try it, swing it. It sounds like the devil is kind of showing off because he's real good with cowboy stuff. I remember a song my grandfather use to sing that is similar to this one. The devils do fancy rope tricks to show off to the ladies. This song is like that because the devil is bragging about being a good cowboy.

Song 12
| | | | | | | | | | | | |
1.
Ñe ña wu li ah ali
2.
I hu wa ñi ba hi wa ku ku ŋo ya
wuli na sai si
3.
Oi go ha wo li yo up ama
wo poi ma na
| | | | | | | | | | | | |

1. Ñeñawul a'al
2. I:ya ñ-bahi ku:giḍ wulid (or wupulṣc=the plural of wulid).
3. Oi g hawuld u:pam wo:po

1. DEVIL KIDS
2. THE END OF MY TAIL IS TIED
3. GO WITH THE KNOT, RETURN RUNNING

These devil kids, they are horses, or cows, and have tails. Their tails are already tied because they were born that way. The horses have knots in their tails and that's what makes them strong, that power is in their tail. We cut that out so they don't buck us off or something.

Song 13

1.	Gesi	wepu	ŋo	ma	po	po	ta	li					
2.	I	hu	wes	an	ñehi	ana	wo	po	hima				
3.	Wa		sa	po	ma	ma	si	mia	wo	po	hi	me	
4.	Wi	ñi	ña	wo	to	mat	ha						

1 Gesi wegi poptolig
2. Ha wes ñeñe'i am wo:po
3. Wa s-ap'e masma wo:po
4. Wijiña wo matog

1. GREAT RED WILD HORSES
2. THEIR SONGS ARE RUNNING
3. THEY LOOK BEAUTIFUL AS THEY GO
4. WITH THE ROPES FRAYING

Jose saw this, or maybe it was someone else who was chasing after those wild horses. Maybe Jose got this song when he was on roundup. Those are wild horses that got away from the cowboys. What the song says to me is that the horses are running, dragging the cowboy's ropes behind them. It is the last phrase that says this about the ropes and how they unravel. Maybe this song didn't come in a dream, but the horses were just singing.

Songs that say cuhug *come at night.* Huḍuñig *comes in the evening, sundown, and you can dream that.* Si'alig *is morning songs, and are also dreamed.* Da:m juk *comes at midday, but these songs come when you're awake. I think this song is one of the* da:m juk *songs. Those horses are singing songs when they run away from the cowboys.*

Song 14

1.											
Gesi	cu	cu	ko	ma	wa	po	kali				
2.											
I	hu	wa	ta	ñe	hi	an	o	wo	po	hi	me
3.											
Wo		sa	po	ma	ma	si	mia	wo	po	hi	me
4.											
Wi	ñi	na	we	to	mi	am					

1. Gesi cuhugam wapkial
2. I:ya ha ñe'i an wo:po hime
3. Wa s-ap masma wo:po hime
4. Wijina tobwig

1. GREAT NIGHTTIME COWBOYS
2. THEIR SONGS ARE RUNNING
3. THEY LOOK BEAUTIFUL AS THEY APPROACH
4. WITH THEIR ROPES TWIRLING

The songs come running with the devil cowboys who are singing them. Jose dreams this. It's really dusty, blowing dust all around. The cowboys can't see very well because it's real windy, like it is on roundup. The cowboys are those devils because us cowboys don't go on roundup after dark. It's like this song chases the previous one.

Song 15

1.											
Ṣoig		ali	wa		kia	li	oi		game		
na		to	ge	gam	hu	ñe	oi	de	ke		
wo	po	hi	me								
2.											
Pia	me	to	ñi	ña	ñe	to	ka	oi	na	ga	mo
ṣu		ṣulo		hi		na	kam				

1. Ṣo'ig ali wapkial oi na:to gmhu ñ-oid k wo:po
2. Pi'am nen'oid k oid gmhu ṣeṣelin hi:nk

1. PITIFUL YOUNG COWBOYS GET READY TO CHASE ME
2. YOU DON'T SEE ME AND GO YELLING

I think an animal sings this about the cowboys who chase and yell at them. You know, like on roundup when the cowboys do all that work. A cow spirit sings this song to the cowboys. I think that the cowboys didn't find this cow and it got away from them.

Song 16

1.	I	ia	wa	ki		gamo	wa		kia	ali			
2.	Oi	ga	mi	tai	wa	ñe							
3.	Ga	je		wa	na	cu	mo	hi	ma				
4.	Cu	wena	wu		siko	cu	mo	hi	ma				

1. I:da mo ki: gamai wakial
2. Oid am tai wañim
3. K jewed ce:mo hima
4. Jewed we:sko ce:mo hima

1. OVER THERE LIVES A COWBOY
2. GO AHEAD AND GO
3. LAND ALL OVER WALKING
4. LAND EVERYWHERE, WALKING

This is about a cowboy at Jose's own village. He probably didn't dream this song, but he learned it from someone else. It talks about the land around the village, the district or maybe even the reservation. That cowboy is out looking for cows on horseback.

Song 17

1.	Gesi	cu	hu	ga	mo	ka	wa	yo					
2.	Gesi	cu	hu	ga	mo	ka	wa	yo					
3.	Ida	wa	ci	ñi	wa	ke	ñe		ḍa	woi	poi	wa	ke
4.	We	si	kuñ	da	gio	ma	ha	mam					

1. Gesi cuhugam kawiyu
2. Gesi cuhugam kawiyu
3. I:da cini k ñ eḍa wui i:bhui
4. Wesko ñ-dagimun

1. GREAT NIGHT HORSE
2. GREAT NIGHT HORSE
3. IT CAME TO ME AND BLEW INSIDE OF ME
4. ALL OVER IT MASSAGED ME

This horse came into his dream. The horse put his mouth on Jose and breathes inside of him and massages him. This horse teaches Jose how to cure people. I think that the horse is curing Jose too. But I don't know what was wrong with him; the song doesn't talk about that.

Song 18

1.												
Gesi	mata		yo	ñe	ka	wa	yo					
2.												
Gesi	mata		yo	ñe	ka	wa	yo					
3.												
Ka	hoi	ka	me		ke	je	ḍo	meme li		ma		
4.												
Ka	oi	ka	me		ke	je	ḍo	ñei	me	lima		
5.												
Ka	hoi	ju		pi	ña							

1 Gesi matai ñ-kawiyu
2. Gesi matai ñ-kawiyu
3. K oidk me:kjeḍ memelim
4. K oidk me:kjeḍ ñe'i melim
5. K ju:piñ

1. MY GREAT ASH-COLORED HORSE
2. MY GREAT ASH-COLORED HORSE
3. FROM FAR AWAY RUNNING
4. FROM FAR AWAY SONG RUNS
5. AND DISAPPEARS IN THE GROUND

That horse, that ash-colored horse, came to him and started singing. I think that this is a morning song, it was gotten in the morning. I don't really understand what it means.

Song 19

1.												
Ñata	ṣa	pa	hi	ma	ta	ma	ka	wa	yo			
ña	wu	li	ṣo	hi	ga							
2.												
Iya	to	ñai	mo	mo	to	ka	ya	ta	ṣa	po		
meko	hi	ma										
3.												
Wañe	ñis	hi		poi	ña		ñe	moi	na			
ṣo	po	li	yo	o		ka						

1. Ñ-i:ya s-ap'e himdam kawiyu ñiawul ṣoiga
2. I:ya ñ-mo:mto'id s-ap me:k hima
3. Wa ñ-i:bena ñ-mui ṣopoliga

1. MY GOOD WALKING HORSE, PET DEVIL
2. WITH A LONG WALK, HE GIVES ME A RIDE
3. MY BREATH WAS SAVED

A horse came and gave Jose a ride, his pet horse. He is really proud of his horse; he is happy. That ride saved his breath so he can do other things like curing.

Song 20

1.												
Gesi	cu		toŋi	ka	wa	yo						
2.												
Gesi	cu		toŋi	ka	wa	yo						
3.												
Ṣaña	ba	no	cu	hi	ga							
4.												
o	mamaga		wa	ko	ko	aŋ	no	si	si	wo	na	
ce	mo		he	ña								
5.												
Gesi	to	tawe	yo	gi	me	li	momotoka		co	taña		

1. Gesi ce:dagi kawiyu
2. Gesi ce:dagi kawiyu
3. Ṣ-ñ cu:ig?
4. Memek ku:git sisiwod ce:wimeḍ
5. Gesi toha hohogimel mo:mtk cuhina

1. GREAT BLUE HORSE
2. GREAT BLUE HORSE
3. WHAT AM I GOING TO DO?
4. DISTANT TIP SPARKLING
5. GREAT WHITE BUTTERFLY RIDES ALL OVER

The horse might give Jose a ride. Sparks come out of the horse's tail, and they go everywhere and see many things. Did the horse give him a ride? I kind of don't know.

Song 21

1.	Ṣa		ñei	si	wa	kiya	li	moño	woi	hi		ma	
2.	Ṣa		ñei	si	wa	kial	li	moño	woi	hi		ma	
3.	Ge	si	cu	cuk	ga	wi	ñi	na		sioi			
4.	Mo	mo	ta	moi	ña	wo	li	hi	mam				

1. Ṣa ñ-wakial wo ñ-wuadam
2. Ṣ ñ-i wakial wo ñ-wuadam
3. Gesi cuk wijina s-oi
4. Mo'o da:m ñiawul him

1. WHY AM I ACTING LIKE A COWBOY?
2. WHY AM I ACTING LIKE A COWBOY?
3. BIG BLACK ROPE
4. ABOVE THE DEVIL'S HEAD WALKING

This reminds me of a song that my late grandpa used to sing. This is about a cowboy riding a horse. He has and is swinging a lariat. But I think that that man Jose is kind of like proud of what he does. He has been learning from the devils to be a good cowboy.

Song 22

1.												
Ce		to	ki	ya	kai	mali	me		kano	ka	ci	
2.												
Ce		to	ki	ya	kai	mali	ma		kano	ka	ci	
3.												
Ku	na	wa	ka	ñe	ña	wul	ai					
ya	a	ha	wui	ñe	io	op	am					

1. Ce:dag akimel me:k ka:cim
2. Ce:dag akimel me:k ka:cim
3. Eḍa g ñeñawul a'ai wui ñe'iopa

1. THE GREAT BLUE WATER DISTANTLY LIES
2. THE GREAT BLUE WATER DISTANTLY LIES
3. AND FROM THERE THE DEVILS RUSH OUT

The water in the song could be the ocean or the Colorado River. I don't really know which it is talking about. The water is where the devils live, like it said in one of the earlier songs.

Song 23

1.												
Ñe	ña	wu	li	wo		po						
2.												
Ñe	ña	wu	li	wo		po						
3.												
Gesi	to	oi	wa	wi	ñi	na						
4.												
Gesi	cucu	ka	wi	ñi	na	pa	wepo	nan				

1. Ñeñawul wo:po
2. Ñeñawul wo:po
3. Gesi o'oi wijina
4. Gesi cuk wijina wepogid

1. THE DEVILS ARE COMING
2. THE DEVILS ARE COMING
3. GREAT SPECKLED ROPE
4. GREAT BLACK ROPE IMITATES

It's the devils, the cowboys, with the ropes. They use them in their job. The black rope imitates the speckled rope. I think it is the devil cowboys who are singing this song. I don't know who dreamed it, maybe Jose, but he probably learned it.

Song 24

1.												
Cu	cuk	no	no	waŋ	ke	no	wake	ñe	ña wul		cumi	
ñei	opa	ki	ma									
2.												
Wa	ñe	si	wa	pai	no	kosi	ba		baki	cum	mia	
mona	hi	me										
3.												
Juña	weḍ	ce	ḍo	ña								

1. Cuk dodoag k ñeñawul ñe'iopa
2. Wa ñ-wainomi k s-ba:bagi mia him
3. Jeweḍ wo ce:mo

1. THE DEVILS EMERGE FROM THE GREAT BLACK MOUNTAIN
2. THE GREAT IRONS COME CLOSE SLOWLY
3. AND COVER THE EARTH

I think that the wainomi *(irons) in that song is maybe a steel-post fence, a roping pen, or it could be the branding irons cowboys use on the job. I think that it's the branding irons. This song talks about a mountain that I kind of don't know a lot about. It is probably that S-cuck Do'ag over by Kelibat Wo'o, by where we go rounding up at times. The song says that the devils come running out of this mountain to put a brand on their cows. I am kind of unsure of what is covering the land; is it devils or the cows?*

Song 25

1.												
Mo	kali	no	ag	ha	ẉus		an	ñi				
2.												
Mo	kali	no	ag	ha	ẉus	an	ñi					
3.												
Ge	taŋ	ñia	wu	li	ta	kaci	mu	mui	ñeñe	hi	me	
4.												
Kuña	mo	nia	ke	wu	si	ma	ci		mam			

1. Mo ali do'ag wu:ṣañ
2. Mo ali do'ag wu:ṣañ
3. Eḍa ñeñawul kc mui ñeñei
4. Kuñ mo jiwia k s-macim

1. FROM THE LITTLE MOUNTAIN THEY EMERGED
2. FROM THE LITTLE MOUNTAIN THEY EMERGED
3. INSIDE, MANY DEVIL SONGS
4. WHERE I ARRIVED AND LEARNED

This song says that devils come out of their home, a little mountain. The devils are singing many songs; they teach the people their songs. Jose learned this song from devil spirits.

Song 26

1.	Ṣoi	gaña	si		ke	li							
2.	Nap	añi		wa		ka	me						
3.	Kuŋi	ñe	we	na	si	si	koli	hio		si	ma		
4.	Ña	moi	ñia	ka	wes		maci		ma				

1. Ṣo'ig ñ-si'ihegi
2. N-ap ñ-wi'ikam
3. K eḍa jeweḍ sikoli hiosig
4. Ñ-ia wes macim

1. MY PITIFUL OLDER BROTHER
2. ARE YOU GOING TO LEAVE?
3. IN THIS LAND OF ROUND FLOWERS
4. FROM OVER THERE I LEARNED

It sounds like the song is saying I'itoi, but I don't think so. I think that it's just an older brother of that man, the I. It is related to the second song that also talks about an older brother. In those flowers he learns songs from the devils. Those flowers say that he is in the shadow of death where ghosts and the dead and devils live, that's in the east.

Song 27

1.	Ga	hu	ñoi	tage	wam		hu	ke		ki	me		
2.	Ga	hu	ñoi	tage	mo	li	na		hi	ma			
3.	Ga	hu	ñoi	tage	wam		hu	ke		ki	me		

1. Gahu ñ-oidam gamhu kekiwa
2. Gahu ñ-oidam mulin
3. Gahu ñ-oidam gamhu kekiwa

1. FROM BEHIND ME IT STANDS
2. FROM BEHIND ME IT BREAKS
3. FROM BEHIND ME IT STANDS

I don't understand this song, because I don't get what's standing behind him and what gets broken. I didn't catch what it says.

Song 28

1.	Wai		no	me	ki		ga	me	ñe	ña	wu	li	
2.	Wai		no	me	ki		ga	me	ñe	ña	wu	li	
3.	Hega	wui	ma	to	ñi	wa	ñe	me	he	na			
4.	Ñi	boi	ta	yo		hu	ŋa						

1. Wainomi ki: gmhu ñeñawul
2. Wainomi ki: gmhu ñeñawul
3. Heg wui ñ-wañimed
4. Ñ-i:bhui ku:g

1. THE DEVIL'S IRON HOUSE
2. THE DEVIL'S IRON HOUSE
3. TOWARDS IT THEY LEAD ME
4. AND MY BREATH IS CALMED

The song talks about a devil's house that was an old miners' house, a tin house. It's over in the mountains somewhere. The miners don't live there anymore, just the devils. It sounds like that man, the I in the song, is kind of scared to go there, but he is OK when he's there because he knows that the devils won't hurt him, but will help him. He calms down.

Song 29

1.											
Ñeña	wu	li	wo		po						
2.											
Ñeña	wu	li	wo		po						
3.											
go	mai	wa	kial	hi	me		hai	wa			
4.											
Gesi	ko	ko	maŋi	wu	pu	lo					
5.											
Ju	we	na	we		siko	ko	ko	mai	wa	ge	

1. Ñeñawul wo:po
2. Ñeñawul wo:po
3. Gamai wakial hime
4. Gesi ko:magi wu:lo
5. Jeweḍ wesko ko:magid

1. DEVILS ARE COMING
2. DEVILS ARE COMING
3. THERE THE COWBOY GOES
4. THE GREAT GREY DONKEYS
5. THE GREYING EARTH

The devils are chasing the donkeys, trying to rope them. The human cowboys follow the devils to where the donkeys are standing. It's like the devils lead the cowboys on a roundup, and the devils are like the cattle bosses.

Song 30

1.												
Wa	ñe	pi	oi		wai	mel	ṣu	liña	mo			
2.												
Wa	ñe	pi	oi		wai	mel	ṣu	liña	mo	si	si	gi

3.
I da ge ñia wu li ñ moi ḍa we mo ñio ka
| | | | | | | | | | | | |

1. Wa ñ pi oi wa ṣelñim
2. Wa ñ pi oi wa ṣelñim si:sigiḍ
3. I:ya ñiawul ñ-i:bdag we:maj ñeok

1. I CAN'T UNDERSTAND
2. I CAN'T UNDERSTAND AS I TOSS AND TURN
3. MY DEVIL HEART, I AM TALKING WITH THEM

I think that Jose is trying to learn a song but he can't quite get it straight, he can't learn it the right way. It makes him toss and turn in his bed. So the devils come to him to teach him, but he still can't do it. So, Jose has a devil heart because he learned a lot from the devils. They came to him a lot. They meet with him and teach him ways to help the people with their curings. His devil heart is like other people who have an owl heart, deer or rabbit, or eagle heart. The animals help teach the man how to do things right. Lots of people get power in this way. He is a devil.

Song 31

| | | | | | | | | | |

1.
Si wo li ge mo okam ma ñia wu li
2.
Hem ho wu pa ka pi mi ha ka
3.
Hem ho wu pa ka pi mi ha ka
| | | | | | | | | | | | |

1. Si:wod g mo'okam ñiawul
2. Hemho wu:ḍa k bihag
3. Hemho wu:ḍa k bihag

1. BUSHY-HAIRED DEVIL
2. THROWS THE ROPE ONCE AND GETS IT
3. THROWS THE ROPE ONCE AND GETS IT

This song says how devils are really good cowboys. They throw the rope once and get the cow, catch the back legs of the cow. With humans, it takes many tries to catch it. That first line of the song is about a cow because they have long and curly hair.

Song 32

1.												
Sial	ŋe	taŋo	ña	hañ	ẹda	wo	po					
2.												
Ali	si	cuk	duŋa		mo	ḍo	wa	ŋe		ke		
3.												
Kuñ ha		si	ñi	jo		haŋ	ñe		da			
4.												
Gam	husi	mel	kona	mo	ke		ka					

1. Si'al ta:gio ñ-eḍa wo:po
2. Al cuk do'ag eḍa wañe
3. K ñ has iju: ñeid
4. Gamhu si me:k mo ke:k

1. TOWARD THE EAST, I RUN INSIDE
2. LITTLE BLACK MOUNTAIN INSIDE I AM LED
3. AND HOW AM I GOING TO SEE IT
4. STANDING OVER THERE, FAR AWAY

This is that little black mountain again where the devils live, where Jose goes to visit and learn. He wants to go there again and learn. But it is really hard for him to get there, it's a long walk from where he is. So, he wonders how he's going to get there. The song asks, "How am I going to get there?" At the mountain he can learn wonderful things. But the devils might come and hurt you, or treat you bad just for nothing. You have to treat them the right way. They might come to you and play a trick on you, and hurt you, make you have an accident, to make fun of you. That means that they don't like you, or they want to give you something and they are just testing you. They can hurt you and then teach you something about their way. But they can just treat you bad for the fun of it.

Song 33

1.											
Ñe	ña	wu	li	ah	ah	ali					
2.											
Cu	hu	ga	ŋi	wesi piwa		kia	wo		pohi	me	
3.											
Si	al	iŋa	wena	do	kosi	piwa			ga		
wo	po	hi	me								

4.
Yu pama ci ñiwa ta ṣai tona liŋ wehe nato
kosi piwa wo po hi me
| | | | | | | | | | | | |

1. Ñeñawul a'al
2. Cuhug ñ wes sisiwani wo:po hima
3. Si'alig we:maj kosimdag wo:po hima
4. U:pam jiwia taṣ tonalig we:hemaj ga:ṣ wo:po hime

1. DEVIL KIDS
2. AT NIGHT I RUN WITH THEM
3. IN THE MORNING I RUN WITH THE SUNRISE
4. I RETURN HOME RUNNING WITH THE SUNLIGHT

The devil kids are leading someone around at sunrise. That takes a person, the patient, away from the east, away from the shadow of death because it's not time for the person to die. That person is close to death during the night but is saved by the devil kids who bring him back home. Those early morning sunshines are like a blessing for the sick, the patient. The shining sun is powerful in cures. This is when the cure is over. I think that Jose kind of got sick from the devils and kind of died. The devils told him that he was not yet ready to die, and those devil kids took him home, they healed him.

Song 34
| | | | | | | | | | | | |
1.
Si ali wa ki me
2.
Si ali wa ki me
3.
Ali wesi nono waŋi nono himo ñia wu li ceno
wa ki me
| | | | | | | | | | | | |

1. Si'alig wa:k
2. Si'alig wa:k
3. Wes dodoag ñiawul c añ wa:k

1. I ENTER IN THE MORNING
2. I ENTER IN THE MORNING
3. I ENTER ALL THOSE DEVIL MOUNTAINS

This is another sunrise song. Jose went into a devil mountain and has been in many of them. In there the devils were scattered around where they live. He went inside to learn from them, or to just visit with them. At this point it wasn't a scary thing to do, and the devils show him where they live.

Song 35

1.												
Si		ali	ke		ki	me						
2.												
Si		ali	ke		ki	me						
3.												
Ta		ṣai	wa	tono	liŋa	je	wena	we		siko		
mamasida												

1. Si'alig ke:k
2. Si'alig ke:k
3. Taṣ tonoliḍ jewed we:sko mamasid

1. SUNRISE STANDING
2. SUNRISE STANDING
3. EVERYWHERE, THE SUNSHINE ILLUMINATES THE LAND

This is the last, the closing, song. The sun rises up and the curing is completed. Jose is just looking around at the desert. All seems clear, bright, and good.

Song Analysis

The songs say that the devils live in mountains, there are horses and cows milling about, the devils are humanlike and work as cowboys, and devils are important sources of power who serve as mentors to humans. They are a poetic version of our previous descriptions. We find the Manol set to be a grand celebration of the cowboy way of life, of roundups, working with livestock, riding horses, and living out in the desert away from home. The songs are silent, however, on the issue of devil sickness, a critique of capitalism, and culture change. Thus, there is not an appreciable difference between Hawk Flying's and Jose Manol's devil songs. Both sets include references to mountains, devils, gaining power, shamanic techniques, and so forth. As one might expect, Manol's set includes more detail and describes more events (riding horses and chasing and roping cattle), characters (horses, cows, cowboys), and locations, indicating the narrative fullness of this long set.

If our theory of primary and secondary poetic tensions is correct, then this set should present the audience with information on who the I, you, and they are. The set should also have an overall narrative moral, an artistic tension and sequencing, that is presented to the audience for contemplation and resolution.

The Manol set is framed, like all long sets, by a series of four evening *(huḍuñig)* songs (1–4) and a series of four morning *(si'alig)* songs (32–35). Framing is a universal feature of O'odham long song-sets, and framing is clear in this set. It is at sunset that a curing *(wusot)* session begins. This moment is explicit in the first framing songs of the set, which describe the evening: "FROM WHERE THE SUN SETS," "WITH THE EVENING NEAR THE SONGS BEGIN," "THE DEVILS APPEARED AS DARKNESS APPROACHED," and "THEIR SONGS SOUND BEAUTIFUL AS EVENING FALLS OVER THE EDGE" denote the important transition from daylight to darkness, the supernatural realm of the curer, the spirit world, the emergence of devils, and the anxiety of the patient. Nighttime curing sessions ideally last all night but often last only four hours or so (Bahr and Haefer 1978, 90). This song-set lyrically suggests that the cure consumes the entire night from sunset to sunrise. (At least, a set of this length could take an entire night to sing.) This is attested to in the final four morning (framing) songs: "TOWARD THE EAST, I RUN INSIDE," "I RETURN HOME RUNNING WITH THE SUNLIGHT," "I ENTER IN THE MORNING," and "EVERYWHERE, THE SUNSHINE ILLUMINATES THE LAND." The framing songs are highly suggestive of time and are the only explicit time representations in this set.

Narrative access into the world of the Manol set is gained through Songs 2 and 26. They are poetic anomalies of a sort because they are unexpected, even surprising, and not identifiable as devil songs per se. For one thing, neither song mentions devils or any other noun subject common to devil songs. For another, an "elder brother" is the distinctive song subject in both. From a classificatory standpoint, neither Song 2 nor Song 26 could be identified by a listener as a devil song if these were heard individually and outside of this song-set's context.

In our thinking, Song 2 refers to the song's I's older brother, the evening, and water. Such references are seemingly anomalous for two reasons. First, the older brother is the primary subject of the song. In a devil song-set, a listener expects things devil-like to be featured (horses, devil kids, ropes, cows, and so on). Why then is the I's older brother emphasized? Second, is this older brother a reference to I'itoi, the man-god creator of the O'odham universe, or to a blood relative? Our conclusion is that it refers to the latter. Linguistic evidence resides in the word *si'ihegi,* which refers to one's older sibling, rather than I'itoi, who is also called Si:s Ma:kai. Further, and more importantly, the I of the song asks a disturbing question: "What happened to my older brother?" The implication is that the I's older brother has gone away from and presumably exposed his younger brother to an apparently threatening and perhaps frightening situation. Did the older brother bring the I to this location? If so, how? And if the older brother did this—as the song implies, though it is left unstated—is it that the I's older brother is deceased and either a ghost *(cukuḍ)* or a devil? The latter is more likely, since this is a set of devil, not owl songs. But ultimately the song is mute on this point.

This song takes us a long way in establishing the primary poetic tension. We conclude that the I is a living human who has a devil for a brother. The tension establishes concern for the predicament the I finds himself in.

The water mentioned in this song is also curious. Is it a reference to the Gulf of California, the ocean, the Colorado River, or possibly a stock pond *(wo'o)* on the reservation? If the ocean, the reference suggests power acquisition in that the ocean is itself inhabited by spirits, including devils, and is a destination of a salt-gathering and power-seeking pilgrimage (Underhill et al. 1979). If a stock pond, then this too is suggestive, since stock ponds are frequented by devils and the devil's animals (cows and horses) because of their association with the cattle-ranching enterprise.

Despite these textual ambiguities, Song 2 sets the stage; it creates a primary poetic tension between the I of the song, presumably the dreamer, and something else. A key to understanding this set lies in answering what this something else is. The best clue is found in Song 1. Here the I of the song is approached by devil kids, who "COVER ME IN FLOWER PETALS" "AS THEY RUN PAST." Viewed sequentially, Song 1 describes an event that was perhaps emotionally unsettling and anxiety provoking for the I (being approached by devil spirits as darkness arrives), and Song 2 elaborates or intensifies this dilemma when the I is abandoned by his older brother, whom the I recognizes as one of the spirits. Thus far, Song 2 with the assistance of Song 1 creates an important literary tension; it generates an intellectual and emotional dilemma. In other words the I, or the subject of the song-set and its unfolding drama, is anxious about being approached by devils, and particularly so when he is left alone by his older brother.

Let's jump ahead and answer how this problem, the I's dilemma, is resolved. For the next and only time, Song 26 returns to the "older brother" subject. A notable shift in tone occurs between Songs 2 and 26. While the I still asks about his older brother, the I has now apparently reached a frame of mind that implies that the devils no longer frighten him. For instance, the I boastfully sings, "FROM OVER THERE I LEARNED." Again the preceding song holds an important clue to the significance of this pivotal song. The statement in Song 25, "I ARRIVED AND LEARNED," marks a notable shift in the I's attitude. It is a striking change, in contrast to the anxious moments of the I in Song 2 and the subdued, muffled boastfulness of Song 26. The act of learning, of obtaining power from devils, resolves the inherent tension Song 2 established. It is as if Song 2 asks, "What am I to do?" while Song 26 answers it by saying, "I'm going to learn." The song does not conclusively resolve the question of what happened to the older brother. It does establish that the older brother is a devil, a devil who has come to meet his younger brother to help him attain curative abilities. This song also, in retrospect, presents this set's secondary poetic tension.

By way of outline, we suggest the following narrative structure for the Manol song-set:

1. Primary Poetic Tension (establishes song subjects; anxiety is created):
    a. The I is abandoned with devils; anxiety created (Songs 1 and 2).
    b. Devils approach the I and offer their power (e.g., Songs 3, 5, 6).
    c. The I (dreamer) is still anxious (e.g., Songs 9, 10).
2. Secondary Poetic Tension (the I subject accepts the tutoring of devils; the I gains knowledge):
    a. Overcomes anxiety; the I learns from the devils (Songs 25, 26).
    b. Through learning, the I is calmed and becomes moderately boastful (confident) of new-found powers and success (e.g., Songs 31, 34).

Songs 1 through 24 detail the coming of devils to the I, but also of ambivalent feelings or apprehension about these visits. Songs 25 through 35 communicate the resolution the I reaches in that the I is now comfortable and calm with the devil visits and tutoring and is in fact actively seeking the devils' company. In Song 28, for instance, the I is led to the "DEVIL'S IRON HOUSE," where his "BREATH IS CALMED." This "iron house" probably refers to a nineteenth-century prospector's tin shack or the metal posts of a corral. Upon arrival at the iron house, the I is apprehensive, yet the I is relieved once he gets there and understands that the devils mean him no harm and are in fact there to teach him about their power and way.

The I receives power from the devils he meets. In the first part of the set, the I begins to receive power (songs, techniques, objects), if tentatively and passively; that is, the I narrates how the devils do something to or for him, but the I does not say whether or not he accepts or even learns from these encounters. The implication is that he does because of the repetition of encounters throughout the set, but there is a distinct modesty in the I's public announcements. The second part of the set provides a transformation on this point. Modest in the first part, he is boastful in the second. The I is no longer a passive recipient of the devils' power. Now the I states clearly and confidently, "I ARRIVED AND LEARNED" (Song 25), "FROM OVER THERE I LEARNED" (Song 26), and "I AM TALKING WITH THEM" (Song 30). These are confident proclamations in that the I is not afraid of the devils; he can learn from them and enter into verbal exchanges with them. The I has become one of them, has become a devil, as is admitted in Song 30, "MY DEVIL HEART." The secondary poetic tension, therefore, is resolved with the I's process of learning from devils fearlessly and with confidence. It is a process whereby a humble human is confronted by spirits who can be dangerous, but who can also benevolently assist the human I in gaining important knowledge.

Lopez said in his commentary on Song 30 that Manol had a "devil heart." Throughout the set, an I receives power from, is tutored by, devils. As we have proposed in the above analysis, the I learns the devils' ways through various means: massage, song, throwing power, use of fetishes or tools *(iagta)*. The devils are benevolent teachers and mentors, and the human, a humble and gracious pupil. Over one half of the way through the set, the pupil becomes confident in the knowledge bestowed upon him. The knowledge and power given by the devils enters into his body and his mind. Techniques are provided to the body through the physical acts of massage, while songs are provided for the mind through the act of singing and subsequent memorization. The devils even aid in the human's memorization of songs. This is found in Song 6, where the devils "throw up" into the I. The word *wipiot,* to vomit, is used in various forms to refer to the act of receiving power from a spirit. To spit *(siswa)* and to teach *(maṣcam)* are also methods used in the transfer of power from spirit to human. This "spit" or "vomit" is said to go into a person's heart and mind so that they won't forget what is learned; it enters into the imagination. It is through a combination of these actions that Manol achieved his devil heart, the location of a shaman's powers.[7]

With a devil heart, Manol recognizes in himself—and others recognize as well—that he is a capable curer of devil sickness. To possess a devil heart is to possess a publicly acknowledged curing ability of devil sickness. Manol's devil heart is his curing credential. His encounters, according to the songs, provide him with a repertoire of song, blowing *(wusot)* technique, and use of devil's tools *(iagta)*. Interestingly, devils give him other, noncuring capabilities as well. For instance, in Song 11 devils teach the I roping techniques, and in Song 29 the devils show cowboys how to round up some donkeys. Song 31 tells of how the devils are really good cowboys because they can lasso running cattle's hind hooves on the first throw (an admittedly difficult maneuver).

Therapeutic Aspects

The preceding analysis of song sequence, structure, and lyric content relates directly to the issue of therapeutic efficacy, something that has not received adequate attention in the literature. First and foremost, efficacy is based and evaluated on how the singing of songs stimulates and pleases the sickness-causing spirit (Bahr et al. 1974). Technically, spirits are the most important audience for singers who perform curing songs, according to the O'odham medical theory. We claim that the overall song-set narrative, the moral of the story and its poetic tensions, also serve a therapeutic purpose. On the one hand, songs are sung directly to and for spirits who hear them, and if pleased by what they hear, they will then release the patient from their illness. On the other hand, a patient and his or her relatives are also an audience. Songs are sung to benefit patients who hear them and who interpret and try to understand the experience and knowledge encapsulated in the haiku-like songs. The difficulty for the patient lies in their grasp of the allusions, metaphors, and analogies that apply to their own struggle to heal their illness.

DL:

Hega'i a:cim a:g wusosig,	About the curing,
mo hab kaij a mo has ma:s e-wua,	what we say that it does,
mat o hema kulañmad, o ha-wuso,	that someone will check, or cure,
"Hascu gawul cu'ig duajida	"What's different about the diagnosis
c wusosig?"	and curing songs?"
Mañ hab a:g mo ha'ic hab cece	Like I said, some say
mat hab o si s-ap i e-ta:tk,	that that will make them feel really fine,
mat hekid g jiawul wo ha-mumkic,	whenever the devil will make them feel sick,
o g cukuḍ wo ha-mumkic,	or if the owl will make them sick,
mat hekid kawiyu wo i ha-wua,	whenever a horse will buck them off,
o g cukuḍ wo ha-mumkic,	or if the owl will make them sick,
mat o ha-nodag,	make them dizzy,
kc mat wo g s-kosim,	and make them sleepy,
c kawiyu wo i wua ha'icu	and the horse will buck them off
wo s-ko'ok,	and will hurt them,
o heba'i wo ha'icu	or something will
wo ha-toskoñ ap ha'ab.	be swollen and sore on them.
T'b'o cei g ma:kai,	And the shaman will say,
"Mo g jiawul mumkidag,"	"It's devil sickness,"
t'o ha-a:g wo e-wuso	and will tell someone to
g jiawul mumkidag.	cure the devil sickness.
Kc t-hab wo juñ k ha'i hab cece	And so they will do it, and some say
mo abṣ wui i gewkṣa g s-ko'ok,	that the pain disappears,
c hab ha'ha e:p i pi s-ko'ok,	and it no longer hurts,
pi-ta:t s-ko'ok.	is no longer painful.

Heg ap mamci mo k mo	That's how they know that it
si wo ha-elidag,	really takes care of them,
ñe'ñe'i wusosig g jiawul ñeñe'i,	singing the devil songs,
c ha'ab mamci o huhugi g toskoñ	they know that the swelling will disappear
c mat p an hab o e-ju:.	and that they are then better.
Ha anai mat p heba'i ha-wua	Their pain went away
kawiyu huhugkaj s-ap ha-ta:tk,	wherever a horse hurt them, and they will feel fine,
c hega'i cukuḍ i ñe'i	and the owl songs
mat am o ha-ñe'icuda	that they will sing for them,
g cu:ckuḍ,	for the owls,
t-kaij c p cece mo'ab	some say this makes them
si s-ap i ha-ta:tk,	feel really well,
c haha pi ha-ko:simcud,	and they are no longer sleepy,
ha-a'apedag ha-mo'o,	and it cures their head,
mat pi hab cu'ig ha-nonḍagcud,	and they are no longer dizzy,
ha-a'ap kc ap'e wohogamcud,	it cures them and that makes sure
mo s-wohom hega'i	that one truly
s-wohogamcud e-ñeñe'i,	believes their songs,
k ha'icu t-mumkidag	some of our sickness
c jumal i s-ko'ok	and brings down the pain and
na:nko ta:tkam,	other odd feelings,
c hab s-ap i ta:tkcud	and the people
g hemajkam.	feel fine.
C no a woho mo s-hoho'id hegam	And is it true that
ha'icu jejawul	those devils
mat o ka: g e-ñeñe'i?	like to hear their songs?
Ñe, s-wohomo,	Look, it is true,
s-hoho'id mat wo ka: g e-ñe'i,	they like to listen to their songs,
heg abṣ s-ap i ha-ta:tk,	and that makes them feel good,
g jejawul s-hoho'id g e-ñe'i,	the devils like their songs,
mat wo ha-kai, cu:ckuḍ,	what they hear, spirits,
ko'o'i, he ha'icu i mumkidag.	rattlesnakes, or other sickness.
Gogogs ha'icu i	Dogs and other ones
s-hoho'id g e-ñe'i.	like their songs too.
Wo kai, k dagito g hemajkam,	They will hear them and will then let the people alone,
wo ha'as mumkic.	and they stop sickening them.
Mo ha'ic abṣ e-wusot e-wustan	Some they just blow and they

pi-am hu'i si s-hoho'id.	don't really like it.
Eḍa ha'ic hega'i si ka	Some really like to listen
map t wo ñe'iculitk	to the singing
k wuso heg si s-hoho'id	and blowing and that's what the
jejawul k ñe'i.	devils really like.
Ha'icu i mo mumkicud,	Other spirits that make you sick,
heg si s-hoho'id	they really like
k ñe'i heg hab wo si	their songs and that really
s-ap i ha-ta:tk,	makes them feel good,
k wo ha-dagito.	and will let them alone.
Ha'icu i cecpa'owi,	Other spirit-ways, like prostitute,
kotdopi, s-hoho'id mat g	jimson weed, they like
e-ñe'i wo kai,	their songs and they will hear them,
wo ha'as	and then they quit making you
mumkic.	sick.

We now turn our attention to how we think that the Manol set provides therapy for patients. In none of the Manol songs is a direct reference made to devil sickness. This absence is not unusual, nor is it a deficiency of this song-set, since no curing songs, to our knowledge, are self-referential in this manner. They do not speak of themselves in the language of sickness and cure. We propose that the therapeutic aspect of this song-set, and presumably other curing-song genres, derives directly from its sequence, structure, the moral of the primary and secondary poetic tensions, its narrative, and the experiences the I has with spirits. Therapy for the patient, therefore, is grounded in allegory and symbol.

A patient is first diagnosed by a *ma:kai,* who identifies the illness-causing way or ways. The shaman then prescribes food and sexual prohibitions and recommends that the patient hire a ritual curer or curers to sing the appropriate songs. As with any *ka:cim mumkidag,* the consequences of neglecting one's health can have tragic results. In other words, obtaining a maximal-level cure is essential for regaining one's health. Personal uncertainty about the illness, if not outright fear of it, drives the patient to seek professional care. But one never really knows if the person who is hired is capable of effecting a cure or even a proper diagnosis, for that matter.

Manol's song-set allegorically, or by what Lévi-Strauss calls abreaction, replicates the uneasiness (the secondary poetic tension) the patient may feel about their illness. Keep in mind that the first half of the Manol set narrates the story of a person who is approached by devils and is apprehensive, if not fearful. This apprehension or fear is similar to what the patient experiences. The patient contracts the devil sickness, experiences symptoms, receives a diagnosis, and hires ritual curers. Through the song-set an allegory between patient and ritual curer is established. The patient is anxious about health, while the curer is, according to the song-set narrative, anxious about his devil encounters. In both cases, devils cause illness or provide an ultimate cure. The song-set offers the alleviation of the patient's fears in the same manner that the song's I's fears are alleviated. In the second half of the song-set, as the narrative progresses, it becomes clearer to the patient, as it did for the song's I, that it is not necessary to fear because the curer's ability to heal is made poetically manifest. The songs reveal to the patient that the curer is powerful because the curer is a good student of the devil's teachings and mentoring. The desired results are forthcoming because the curer has the ear of his devil mentors.

This theory parallels or is similar to the hypothesis forwarded by Claude Lévi-Strauss (1967). He hypothesized that a shaman (or ritual curer) creates a series of correspondences—abreactions—between patient and shaman and between audience and shaman. This was forwarded in his classic article, "The Sorcerer and His Magic." Briefly stated, he hypothesized that "the type of abreaction specific to each shaman . . . might symbolically induce an abreaction of his own disturbance in each patient" (Lévi-Strauss 1967, xx). He argues that there is a complementarity at work in that what the shaman or curer has experienced in his process of gaining curative powers, often a terrifying apprenticeship to spirits, is now reenacted in song, oration, and ritual for the benefit of a patient and audience to reassure them. Anxiety, fear, and other experiences are encapsulated in songs—the historic encounters of the shaman or curer—and are replayed (sung) for the patient's benefit.

Conclusion

In many ways this chapter offers a poetic capsule of the entire book. Songs are the tones that harmonize the concepts and interpretations presented.

We have forwarded a structuralist theory of O'odham curing songs that suggests their sequence and narrative structure are based on two interrelated themes: primary and secondary poetic tensions. Our analysis suggests that efficacy for the patient is a kind of allegorical empathy, what Lévi-Strauss called abreaction. For patients, curing song-sets are an allegorical healing music, a shamanic picture poetry that uses words and music to paint pictures of the spirit world. We are reluctant to say firmly that all O'odham curing song-sets possess these theoretical constructs, but we believe that they do.

We are happy to say that devil songs are conceptually, substantively, musically, and historically of a piece. There is nothing that would signal to an O'odham listener that Hawk Flying's and Jose Manol's devil songs were recorded three-quarters of a century apart. This demonstrates the resiliency of this oral literature and its continued importance and applicability in people's lives.

Several characteristics have remained constant in this genre, according to the songs we have analyzed. First, cowboys continue to predominate as song subjects. Human cowboys are led on journeys by devils to devil homes and around the desert landscape. Both human cowboys and devils participate in cowboy-related activities in these song journeys: they ride horses, chase and round up cattle, brand and eartag livestock, have rodeos, and so on. Second, cattle and horses populate these songs. They are the subjects of the human cowboys' and devils' attention and admiration. Livestock are their playthings and work focus. Third, as a shamanic poetry, the songs tell of, and are the source for, medical inspiration and technical knowledge for humans.

Unlike devil folklore, such things as money, wealth distinctions, and class divisions are entirely absent in devil song-poetry. This music does not speak to such mundane matters. Devil songs transcend the human world of buying and selling, and envy and jealousy. Devil songs derive from the spirit world and are unconcerned with such human trivialities.

Nor can it be argued that devil songs serve as a critique of a cash and wage-labor economy brought about by the very industry that this music celebrates. In this way O'odham devil songs are not a poetics of resistance to capitalism or colonialism. This is not to say that devil song-poetry is unmindful of the dramatic economic and social changes of the time. The songs are, after all, grounded directly within those changes. To find such a critique, one must listen to the stories people tell of devil way. Devil songs calmly overlook the problem of money, of cattle sale for profit, and of the incipient class division in a uniquely O'odham manner. Devil songs, as curative song-poetics, speak a medical language, not one of politics, economics, or resistance.

Finally, devils in the O'odham historical imagination reveal larger historical processes contained in song. The songs are modest statements about a new era in O'odham life and tradition. They are a celebration of the O'odham way. Devil songs share information about the spirit world that sheds light and understanding about the "hard staying land" *(ka:cim jeweḍ)* that today's O'odham call home. And it is in song-poetics, tucked in allegories, metaphors, and symbols, that the O'odham treasure as a storehouse of their historical and mythical imagination.

Conclusion: The Bedeviled Imagination

Devils have hounded the Christian imagination for nearly two millennia. Defined as quintessentially evil, the devil who occupies the imagination is often feared and loathed. The devil and God are thought to be in an eternal battle over souls. The devil personifies all that the Christian detests of the immoral and degraded state of the human condition.

As is well known, the European conquest of the Western Hemisphere was at least partly predicated on or justified by the eradication of the devil, thought to be in residence among the so-called pagan populations. Missionaries supposedly found evidence of the devil's work and influence at every turn, and no evidence was clearer than that embodied in the shaman. One might even say that the missionaries were infatuated with the devil and believed they had found him among the native populations. Unfortunately for many people, the belief in the devil's presence justified conquest by any means available.

Devil beliefs were imparted to native communities by missionaries where indigenous peoples selectively incorporated the beliefs into their cosmologies. Rarely, if ever, did Christian devil beliefs get adopted without significant modification in form, content, and meaning. It appears, for instance, that native devil beliefs did not relegate the devil to the position of great evil and arbiter of tough justice. Rather, the devil or devils did both beneficial and malicious, even precocious, things, not dissimilar to the behavior of the Southwest Coyote trickster figure. At another extreme, and in many cases, the devil came to be viewed as part of the oppressive apparatus of conquest itself. Devils were described and depicted as the possessors of great wealth, those who jealously and vindictively controlled resources. This depiction of devils bore a striking and suspicious likeness to European colonizers, including missionaries. Yet, in still other conceptualizations, the devil came to be viewed or perceived in native communities as themselves (Taussig 1987). Some, like the O'odham, accepted the idea that they were the devils that the missionaries had preached that they were. This did not, however, necessarily mean that they thought of themselves as evil. Rather, the acceptance of the devil designation perhaps provided a way to resist the very institutions that oppressed them as individuals and as communities.

Devils in the Western and O'odham historical imaginations pose interesting questions for both the anthropological and the O'odham communities. But the questions are interesting to each community for far different reasons. For anthropologists, questions revolve around what devils symbolize and mean in indigenous communities. Questions of syncretistic beliefs, history, resistance, gender inequalities, envy, jealousy, and a critique of capitalism come to mind. In many ways these questions are meant to speak to and about Christian beliefs, about Western civilization. For O'odham the questions are related to a sense of self, culture, ethnic association, and the place of myth and history as it connects to the influences of Christianity and capitalism. In a gross simplification, for anthropologists devils present questions of empiricism, interpretation, and comparison; for O'odham they are questions of faith and identity. These differences should not mean, however, that anthropologists and O'odham cannot discuss and learn from one another, that we are destined to forever talk past one another because what we want to know or believe is at odds. Curiosity, after all, is not a monopoly held by either anthropologists or O'odham. Rather, if interested and engaged persons can openly discuss, debate, contest, question, agree, agree to disagree, and above all else, be respectful of other perspectives and modes of knowing and knowledge, then we all have much to gain. Certainly this willingness to agree as well as to contest has been at the heart of our collaborative efforts and has guided the spirit of representation in this book.

Methodologically and theoretically we have tried to chart a course of our own—sometimes as a team, sometimes as individuals—through the process of reducing into writing what we think we know about devil way. Collaboration has sustained us through the research, transcription, translation, interpretation, and analytic processes. Our collaborative labors have resulted in a coauthored document that has attempted to build a bridge between our own voices and between the voices of others heard in this work. The dialogue, the conversation, is not complete, nor will it ever be. This is not a pitfall of this work. And as most conversations go, there are always omissions both for reasons of judgment and out of incomplete knowledge.

The writing of ethnography, primarily with regard to questions of representation and authority, has received much-needed attention in the last decade or so. These important disciplinary correctives have raised issue, among other things, over rhetorical strategies, the use and abuse of scientific language and assumptions, and the situated nature of knowledge claims and issues regarding the essentialization of "culture." The positive outcome of this writerly soul-searching has led anthropology in new and exciting directions and raised new possibilities. Our contribution to the developments in representation strategies is modest and hinges on the theoretical issues of audience and collaborative text production. Early on in our work together, we discussed who we envisioned our audiences to be. And because our respective audiences are in many ways very different, we had the problem of talking between while talking to each audience simultaneously. In retrospect, the results are not fully satisfactory to us. This is because by writing against the conventional writing strategy of the single, authorial voice, ours at times sounds more like a disharmonious chorus of several voices. Furthermore, a problem with this rhetorical strategy is that some sections are too easy for some readers and too difficult for others. For instance, some non-native anthropologists will have found the O'odham-English texts or song analysis disorienting, while some O'odham will have been nonplussed over the theoretical arguments. In trying to please everyone through a constructed and mediated "middle ground" or "bridge," we run the risk of pleasing no one, except perhaps ourselves. The middle ground or bridging dialogue we have pursued was constantly in a state of flux or movement as our envisioned audience's demands forced us into negotiation and compromise.

Despite these potential limitations, we remain committed to coauthorship because it seems to be both an intellectually productive and a personally satisfying avenue through which academic and indigenous representational concerns and knowledge can begin to be balanced. Coauthorship provides a method of subverting the hegemony of one-sided, outsider-generated interpretations, of subverting the representational asymmetries, while balancing the responsibility for saying something about the world between two or more authors, indigenous and anthropological.

Beyond the theoretical issues related to writing, several conceptual constructs were deployed in this work. Political economy provided a way to understand the historic and economic foundation for examining the context in which O'odham devil way developed. The devil as multivocalic symbol of the economic transformation from hunting-gathering-agriculture to wage labor and capitalism is evidenced throughout the New World and is present in the O'odham experience. Issues of envy, jealousy, a two-class division, sorcery, and the perils of possessive self-interest and individualism are certainly aspects of O'odham devil way. In both the Christian tradition and O'odham devil way, ambiguity exists over the person who is wealthy as questions and doubts arise concerning their moral character. We believe that O'odham devil-lore speaks to these issues with eloquence.

The data for this work—devil stories and devil songs—needed to be clearly distinguished when making theoretical claims. On the basis of devil-lore it is plausible to make a cultural Marxist argument similar to Taussig's (1980). The devil does serve as a symbol for the economic transformation experienced by indigenous people as they are brought into a wage-labor market. Moreover, money is problematized and often imbued with an (im)moral character of its own. We diverge from this type of analysis where the O'odham are more inclined to think poorly of wealthy cattle ranchers because the person is stingy or has neglected sacred or secular community responsibilities. It is not monetary wealth alone that identifies the person as immoral. When we turn to devil songs as data, is it still possible to make the analytic association between money and capitalism, and its culturally perceived immorality? Do devil songs, like devil stories, provide evidence of a critique of capitalism, as in Taussig's argument? We do not think that devil songs can bear such a claim. Contrary to early expectations, we found political economy ill-equipped and incapable of providing a meaningful or accurate explanation of what devil songs say. Rather than finding resistance or critique in lyric content, we had to return to the songs to listen carefully to what they had to tell us. It was not until a later draft of this book that we opted for a structuralist orientation for analytic insight into devil songs.

The songs told us several things. The necessity of arranging songs into sets meant that songs are meaningful only when combined by a singer into an overall narrative structure. We believe that song-set arrangement is a theoretical principle used by O'odham ritual curers. Bahr and Haefer (1978) have discussed this important principle and demonstrated how songs are like chapters in a book as they present an unfolding narrative. We further suggested that song-set sequence and structure are guided by two theoretical principles we called primary and secondary poetic tensions. The primary tension establishes the song-set's characters and the relationships that link them together, and the secondary poetic tension then poses a philosophical question or dilemma to be contemplated and perhaps resolved by the patient and others who happen to be in the audience. This question of dilemma is meant to be unsettling when the patient, for example, is put into the shoes of the song-set's I character (the singer). The patient "relives" what the song's I lived in the spirit world. Lévi-Strauss calls the affects of this secondary poetic tension an "abreaction." He suggests that abreaction is a universal healing technique used by shamans everywhere. These theoretical concerns successfully apply in the treatment of O'odham staying sickness because the song-set and its singer(s) replicate the process that the ill person is experiencing. The ritual curer provides a mirror for the patients to see themselves in the song-set narrative. The set's success is its ability to get the ill person to empathize with or live vicariously through what the singer has experienced and is "saying" in lyric content.

Finally, we believe that the most important overall contribution this book makes is in the area of devil-song poetics as literature and literature as culture history. We have attempted to show how O'odham oral literature is a dynamic aspect of culture and history. In addition to its compelling literary achievements and its musical theory, O'odham devil songs as oral literature serve as a register for and barometer of social change, but they also provide a reliable means for contending with the disruptions caused by that change. It is at this point that the difference between everyday forms of devil stories and divinely inspired devil songs crystallizes (and hence the need for a different theory). Devil stories give expression to the human world where conflicts, hostilities, jealousies, and envies associated with economic and social change arise, whereas devil songs calmly, modestly, and provocatively resolve these human matters in the ritual cure context. Conflict, envy, jealousy, and hostility circulate in gossip and stories, and moral evaluations of people's behavior are made and judgments passed. These informal modes of talk are sometimes standardized into devil-lore—those extreme occurrences of gross breaches of appropriate personal behavior. Devil songs, on the other hand, are a curative poetics, divinely conceived, that exist to heal the rifts, the extreme occurrences, that happen between people. In the meantime, devils continue to populate the O'odham reservation, people continue to get devil sickness, and devils continue to contact humans in the land of dreams, spirits, and the phantasmic.

Notes

Introduction

1. The tribe officially changed its name from Papago (a Spanish derived term) to Tohono O'odham in 1982. Tohono O'odham means the "desert people." We will use Tohono O'odham, O'odham, and Papago interchangeably throughout this book.
2. The "-person" of animal, bird, insect, and natural phenomenon refers to the O'odham understanding that such entities or spirits, who inhabit the mythic realm, are proto-humans.

1. Writing about Devil Talk

1. Note that O'odham plurals are frequently created via the reduplication of the first syllable of the word. The plural of *ñe'i* ("song"), for example, is *ñeñe'i*.
2. Kozak prefers this term to emphasize that one of Lopez's stated reasons for working on this project was that he wished to teach the younger generations about this dangerous sickness. Didactic essay is conceptually distinct from "traditional" O'odham verbal genres of song and oratory.
3. The unequal relations between anthropologist and informant has received a good deal of necessary critical attention. As Evers and Molina (1987, 9) point out, the historical relations between investigators and investigated are fraught with hierarchical and unequal power relations.
4. There is a growing body of ethnographic literature that takes seriously the production of egalitarian, collaboratively produced texts. Notable among these efforts are Bahr et al. (1974), Bahr et al. (1995), Cruikshank (1988, 1990a, 1990b), Evers and Molina (1985, 1992), Underhill et al. (1979), and Vander (1986, 1988). The shared promise in these works is that in each case a native person or persons works closely with an academic person to produce texts and interpretations that are culturally sensitive and insightful—significant contributions to the advancement of egalitarian,

multicultural knowledge. In each case interpretation derives from the words of the native contributors rather than from theories of culture and explanation. They are important works that contribute to the cultures from which they derive as well as to the academy. It is to these collaborative efforts that our work aspires.

2. History of Cattle, History of Devils

1. One Villagers, the Akimel O'odham, or more commonly known as Pima, lived in permanent year-round villages along the Salt and Santa Cruz Rivers. Their cultivation practices were more reliable and productive due to a steady and reliable water supply. No Villagers lived in the forbidding desert west of the Tohono O'odham. They were nomadic and are called the Hia Ceḍ O'odham or Sand Papago. They did not build permanent dwellings but were forced into a nomadic lifestyle due to the extremely dry conditions in this part of the Sonoran Desert. Sand Papago hunted and gathered, and worked for produce in the fields of the One Villagers and Two Villagers.
2. In contrast, Castetter and Bell (1942, 56) estimated the One Village Pima, with a more reliable and plentiful source of water, obtained approximately 60 percent of their diet from agriculture.
3. The power and importance of the gift functions at both the individual and group level. As Hyde (1983, 74–76), following Mauss, has observed, the gift establishes bonds of affection between individuals, friends, and family. But "gift exchange at the level of the group [also] offers equilibrium and coherence" (Hyde 1983, 74). This is similar in kind to Pierre Bourdieu's (1984) concept of symbolic capital.
4. This was the final land acquisition by the U.S. of Mexican real estate. The purchase consisted of approximately the lower quarter of the Territory of Arizona.
5. The last major battle was the Camp Grant Massacre in 1871, where an alliance of Anglos, Mexicans, and Pimans attacked and decimated an Apache *ranchería* (Sheridan 1988, 164).
6. A Presbyterian boarding school was established near Tucson and was attended by some O'odham from the Topawa and San Miguel area. By 1912 a Presbyterian school was built in San Miguel. A political and religious split between Catholics and Protestants occurred at this time. A group called the Good Government League, composed of Presbyterian O'odham, were opposed to the more traditionally minded and Catholic League of the Papago Chiefs. The more successful large cattle owners tended to be Presbyterian and members of the Good Government League (Spicer 1962).

7. We have not been able to secure livestock data for the 1980s and 1990s. Although annual counts are being made, the reports are not made publicly available.

3. O'odham Cosmology and Devil Way

1. Bahr (n.d.b) has raised some question as to the antiquity of this ceremony. He argues that it is largely a post-contact, post–nineteenth-century, Christian-influenced ritual. He suggests that it possesses attributes of the Yaqui Easter passion play and the Yuman Keruk (mourning) ceremonies. Bahr feels that the sharing is the result of missionization and close proximity. It has been discussed in some detail by Bahr (n.d.b, 1991a), Galinier (1991), and Underhill (1946). Refer also to Hayden (1987), which includes color drawings of relevant features, and Fontana (1987).
2. This is a wine-drinking ceremony. Participants ferment and drink a wine made from the juice of ripe saguaro cactus fruits. The ceremony is to invoke rain from the four directions to visit their fields. Drunkenness is the desired state and, due to the wine's emetic quality, drinkers vomit the wine. Underhill (1946, 67) noted that the person who vomits is "throwing up the clouds." A symbolic referent is drawn between the violence of vomiting and thunderstorms, both of which moisten the parched earth (see also Waddell 1975, 1976).
3. We have heard young men speak of eagle killing, but we know of no one who has accepted the rigors of this pursuit for power. This of course does not mean that it has not happened recently, only that we are not sure if it has.
4. *Sasantos* is an interesting linguistic amalgamation of three languages. *Santo* is Spanish for saint. *Sasanto* is the plural form of "saint" in O'odham usage. *Sasantos* adds a final */s/,* conforming to the English method of pluralizing.
5. O'odham shamans are not priests in any conventional sense of that term, but O'odham shamans do perform versions of Christian sacraments in the diagnostic session, in addition to their own native sacraments. The use of holy water and crossing the patient are Christian imports into native practice (see chapter 4). In this way it could be said that O'odham shamans emulate Catholic priests, while not being priestly.
6. The importance and significance of dreaming for the O'odham is well documented (Russell 1908; Underhill 1946; Bahr et al. 1974). The dream culture phenomenon extends far beyond the O'odham. For example, consult Kroeber (1925) on Mohave dream life, Spier (1933) on Maricopa, and Park (1938) for a general overview and comparison of Indian dream culture in the U.S. West. For good reviews of the guardian spirit complex,

consult Benedict (1923) and Underhill (1948). This list is by no means exhaustive but is meant to offer a basic review of the centrality and importance of dream in this region.

7. This is not an original observation of ours. The literature on shamanism worldwide reveals how widespread this correlation is.

4. *Jiawul Mumkidag:* Devil Sickness

1. The stratification, or layering, of numerous sicknesses in the body is common. It is common for a person to contract numerous staying sicknesses over the course of his or her lifetime. When stratified, diagnosis is more difficult, since the ways may confuse the shaman's attempts to "see" the illness.

5. Devil Songs and the Cure of Devil Sickness

1. Bahr (1983a) classifies O'odham song-sets according to the number of songs linked by a singer in a set. Hawk Flying's devil songs, for example, comprise what Bahr would call a "short set." A short set is between three and five songs long, which tell of a single episode and provide a brief, terse message. Manol's devil songs comprise a "long set." Long sets are composed of between six and thirty-six songs, are also sung in a fixed sequence, and tell an episodic and unfolding story. Individual songs offer new insights and information on the overall narrative structure of the song-set. A "superlong set" is composed of several long sets that are fixed into an overall sequence comprising an epic narrative. Superlong sets are sung over several separate occasions.
2. Our conclusion parallels Bahr et al.'s (1979, 246) finding that the songs Russell (1908) published are of a piece with current Pima and O'odham song-poetics. They state that the "Pima curing songs of 1902" are the "products of the same literary, music, and culture" as today's O'odham curing songs.
3. Chromaticism (Lévi-Strauss 1964) as a symbol of the spirit world is found throughout the New World. The metaphor or symbol of flowers and the flower world, for instance, is a chromaticism unique to the U.S. Southwest and Mesoamerica (Hill 1992).
4. Jose Manol. This biography of Jose Manol was written by Donald Bahr in March 1994:

> I first met Manol around 1974 when he was summoned to sing a Buzzard cure for David Lopez's uncle Sylvester. David's father Baptisto and I attended that cure, and I tape recorded it.
>
> Manol lived in Ak Chin, about five miles from Santa Rosa. He was well known

for his broad knowledge of curing songs. It was said that he knew distinct songs for every kind of Papago Indian sickness, sometimes just a few songs and sometimes many.

Over the next three or four years I visited Manol to learn how many kinds of songs he knew. Each time I would say, "Do you know songs for [some] sickness, e.g., for Dog or Mouse or Rabbit or even Beaver?" he would nearly always say "yes," and he would then sing the songs.

He is the "Havier" of the Bahr, Giff, and Havier paper cited above. (He used two names, Jose Manol and Manuel Havier. Perhaps the second was his legal, tribally registered name while the first was what most people called him.) Besides the Deer and Cow songs of that paper and the Devil songs here, only one other of Manol's song sets has been printed, namely the eight Ocean songs that were published by me in 1991.

Something was said of Manol in each of the earlier printings. He moved to Comobabi village in the 1980s and died there in the middle or late 1980s. I did not go there to see him although I often vaguely planned to do so. His daughter Sally took care of him in his old age. He loved to sing and did not like to talk—he preferred singing. He was not the least stingy with his songs and always amazed one with how easily he could summon up all of what he knew of even the most obscure type. Altogether I must have recorded about 200 or 250 songs from him, for about 30 kinds of sickness. These 35 devil songs were the most that he knew for any type of sickness. I never asked how many kinds of songs he knew and never asked to record the same kind twice. I am sure he knew more kinds of songs than I recorded, but I believe—because he said so—that he sang all of the songs that he knew of each given type. Each time they came out in an order that makes sense in the manner that the order of these Devil songs make sense.

I wrote all of the recorded songs down more or less in the manner that these Devil songs are written, and I deposited copies of the tapes at the Southwest Musical Archive at Arizona State University. Another set of copies is at the American Philosophical Society in Philadelphia.

5. A maximal-level cure refers to the act of singing the appropriate songs for a sickness that was diagnosed by a shaman. This can be compared with a minimal-level cure whereby a fetish, *iagta,* is applied to the patient's body by the patient or someone else. For example, a horse-tail brush could be applied in an effort to rid a person of devil sickness. If this fails to cure the patient, songs are then required. An account of the distinction between minimal and maximal can be found in Bahr et al. (1974).
6. Examples of devil songs can be found in the work of Francis Densmore and Ruth Underhill. The ethnomusicologist Densmore (1929, 99–101) included a short set of four devil songs in her work on O'odham music. Though she provided English translations and musical annotation, she did not include O'odham language originals. Ruth Underhill (1946, 292–93)

published a short set of five devil songs. This set was sung by Juan Lopez, the shaman grandfather of David Lopez. Again, no O'odham song language is provided. However, Underhill's English versions are superior to Densmore's because Underhill provides what appear to be line-for-line translations rather than narrative paragraphs, as in Densmore's work.

7. People are known to have eagle, turtle, or owl hearts, among others, meaning that the person has been extensively tutored and mentored by one of these spirit entities. It is safe to say that any animal spirit that causes a staying sickness is a potential power source for an O'odham. A person who possesses such a heart is known as a meeter of that spirit (see Underhill 1946).

References Cited

Alonso, Ana María. 1990. "Men in 'Rags' and the Devil on the Throne: A Study of Protest and Inversion in the Carnival of Post-Emancipation Trinidad." *Plantation Society in the Americas,* 73–120.

Appadurai, Arjun. 1986. "Global Ethnoscapes: Notes and Queries for a Transitional Anthropology." In *Recapturing Anthropology,* ed. R. Fox. Santa Fe: School of American Research Press.

Bahr, Adelaide. n.d. "The Spanish Songs of Papago Indians." Manuscript in author's possession.

Bahr, Donald. 1964. "Santa Rosa, Arizona." Manuscript in the Arizona State Museum, Tucson.

———. 1975. *Pima and Papago Ritual Oratory: A Study of Three Texts.* San Francisco: Indian Historian Press.

———. 1983a. "A Format and Method for Translating Songs." *Journal of American Folklore* 96 (380): 170–82.

———. 1983b. "Pima and Papago Social Organization." In *Handbook of North American Indians,* ed. W. C. Sturtevant. Vol. 10, *Southwest.* Washington, D.C.: Smithsonian Institution Press.

———. 1986a. "Pima-Papago -ga: 'Alienability.'" *International Journal of American Linguistics* 52 (2): 161–71.

———. 1986b. "Pima Swallow Songs." *Cultural Anthropology* 1 (2): 171–87.

———. 1988a. "Pima-Papago Christianity." *Journal of the Southwest* 30 (2): 133–67.

———. 1988b. "La modernisation du chamanisme pima-papago." *Recherches Amérindiennes au Quebec* 18 (2–3): 69–81.

———. 1991a. "Papago Ocean Songs and the Wi:gita." *Journal of the Southwest* 33 (4): 539–56.

———. 1991b. "A Grey and Fervent Shamanism." *Journal de la Société des Americanistes* 77:7–26.

———. n.d.a. "Musical Poems in America." Manuscript in author's possession.

———. n.d.b. "Easter, Keruk, and Wi:gita." Manuscript in author's possession.

Bahr, Donald, Joseph Giff, and Manuel Havier. 1979. "Piman Songs on Hunting." *Ethnomusicology* 23 (2): 245–96.

Bahr, D., J. Gregorio, D. Lopez, and A. Alvarez. 1974. *Piman Shamanism and Staying Sickness.* Tucson: University of Arizona Press.

Bahr, Donald, and Richard Haefer. 1978. "Song in Piman Curing." *Ethnomusicology* 22 (1): 89–122.

Bahr, D., L. Paul, and V. Joseph. 1997. *Ants and Orioles: Showing the Art of Pima Poetry.* Salt Lake City: University of Utah Press.

Bahr, D., J. Smith, W. Allison, and J. Hayden. 1995. *The Hohokam Chronicles.* Berkeley: University of California Press.

Bahre, Conrad, and Marlyn Shelton. 1996. "Rangeland Destruction: Cattle and Drought in Southwestern Arizona at the Turn of the Century." *Journal of the Southwest* 38 (1): 1–22.

Bauer, Rolf. 1971. "The Papago Cattle Economy: Implications for Economic and Community Development in Arid Lands." In *Food, Fiber and Arid Lands,* ed. William McGinnies, B. Goldman, and P. Paylore. Tucson: University of Arizona Press.

Behar, Ruth. 1987. "Sex and Sin: Witchcraft and the Devil in Late-Colonial Mexico." *American Ethnologist* 14 (1): 34–54.

Beiber, Ralph. 1938. *Cooke's Journal of the March of the Mormon Battalion, 1846–1847.* Southwest History Series 7. Glendale, CA: Clark.

Benedict, Ruth. 1923. *The Concept of the Guardian Spirit in North America.* Memoirs of the AAA No. 29. Menasha, WI.

BIA (Bureau of Indian Affairs, Papago Agency). 1974. *Range and Livestock Report to the Papago Council.* Sells, AZ: Papago Agency.

Bolton, Herbert. 1932. *Padre on Horseback.* San Francisco: Sonora Press.

———. 1948 [1919]. *Kino's Historical Memoir of Pimeria Alta.* 2 vols. Berkeley: University of California Press.

Bordieu, Pierre. 1984. *Distinction.* Cambridge: Harvard University Press.

Castetter, Edward, and Willis Bell. 1942. *Pima and Papago Indian Agriculture.* Albuquerque: University of New Mexico Press.

Cervantes, Fernando. 1994. *The Devil in the New World.* New Haven: Yale University Press.

Chesky, Jane. 1943. *The Nature and Function of Papago Music.* Master's thesis. Tucson: University of Arizona.

Chevalier, Jacques. 1987. "The Chevalier-Taussig Debate: Who Will Rise to the Bate?" *Social Analysis* 21:92–100.

Clifford, James. 1986. "On Ethnographic Allegory." In *Writing Culture,* ed. J. Clifford and G. Marcus. Berkeley: University of California Press.

———. 1988. *The Predicament of Culture.* Cambridge: Harvard University Press.

Clotts, H. V. n.d. "Nomadic Papago Surveys and Investigations, 1914–1915." Copy on file at Arizona State Museum Library, Tucson.

Crain, Mary. 1991. "Poetics and Politics in the Ecuadorian Andes: Women's Narratives of Death and Devil Possession." *American Ethnologist* 18 (1): 67–89.

———. 1994. "Opening Pandora's Box: A Plea for Discursive Heteroglossia." *American Ethnologist* 21 (1): 205–10.

Crosswhite, Frank. 1980. "The Annual Saguaro Harvest and Crop Cycle of the Papago, with Reference to Ecology and Symbolism." *Desert Plants* 2 (1): 1–62.

Cruikshank, Julie. 1988. "Myth and Tradition as Narrative Framework: Oral Histories from Northern Canada." *International Journal of Oral History* 9 (3): 198–214.

———. 1990a. "Getting the Words Right: Perspectives on Naming and Places in Athapaskan Oral History." *Arctic Anthropology* 27 (1): 52–65.

———. 1990b. *Life Lived Like a Story.* Lincoln: University of Nebraska.

Crumrine, N. Ross. 1977. *The Mayo Indians of Sonora: A People Who Refuse to Die.* Tucson: University of Arizona Press.

Densmore, Frances. 1929. *Papago Music.* Bureau of American Ethnology, Bulletin 90. Washington, D.C.

Ede, Lisa, and Andrea Lunsford. 1984. "Audience Addressed/Audience Invoked: The Role of Audience in Composition Theory and Pedagogy." *College Composition and Communication* 35:155–71.

Edelman, Marc. 1994. "Landlords and the Devil: Class, Ethnic, and Gender Dimensions of Central American Peasant Narratives." *Cultural Anthropology* 9 (1): 58–93.

Evers, Larry, and Felipe Molina. 1987. Yaqui Deer Songs—Maso Bwikam: A Native American Poetry. Tucson: University of Arizona Press.

———. 1992. "The Holy Dividing Line: Inscription and Resistance in Yaqui Culture." *Journal of the Southwest* 34 (1): 3–106.

Finnegan, Ruth. 1992. *Oral Poetry.* Bloomington: Indiana University Press.

Fontana, Bernard. 1976. "Desertification of Papagueria: Cattle and the Papago." In *Desertification: Process, Problems, Perspectives,* ed. P. Paylore and R. Haney Jr. Tucson: Office of Arid Lands Studies, University of Arizona.

———. 1983. "Pima and Papago: Introduction." In *Handbook of North American Indians,* ed. W. C. Sturtevant. Vol. 10, *Southwest.*

———. 1987. "The Vikita: A Biblio History." *Journal of the Southwest* 29 (3): 259–72.

Friedlander, Judith. 1990. "Pacts with the Devil: Stories Told by an Indian Woman from Mexico." *New York Folklore* 16 (1–2): 25–42.

Galinier, Jacques. 1991. "From Montezuma to San Francisco: The Wi:gita Ritual in Papago (Tohono O'odham) Religion." *Journal of the Southwest* 33 (4): 486–538.

Godoy, Ricardo. 1985. "Bolivian Mining." *Latin American Research Review* 20 (1): 272–77.

Griffith, James. 1974. "Franciscan Chapels on the Papagueria, 1912–1973." *Smoke Signal* 30 (fall): 234–55.

———. 1975. "The Folk Catholic Chapels of the Papagueria." *Pioneer America* 7 (2): 21–36.

———. 1979. "Waila—The Social Dance Music of the Indians of Southern Arizona: An Introduction and Discography." *JEMF Quarterly* 15:193–204.

Gross, Daniel. 1983. "Fetishism and Functionalism: The Political Economy of Capitalist Development in Latin America." *Comparative Studies in Society and History* 25:694–702.

Gunst, Marie L. 1930. "Ceremonials of the Papago and Pima Indians, with Special Emphasis on the Relation of the Dance to Their Religion." Master's thesis. Tucson: University of Arizona.

Hackenberg, Robert. 1983. "Pima and Papago Ecological Adaptations." In *Handbook of North American Indians,* ed. W. C. Sturtevant. Vol. 10, *Southwest.* Washington, D.C.: Smithsonian Institution Press.

Haefer, Richard. 1981. "Musical Thought in Papago Culture." Ph.D. diss., University of Illinois, Champaign-Urbana.

Harris, Olivia. 1982. "The Dead and the Devils among the Bolivian Laymi." In *Death and the Regeneration of Life,* ed. M. Bloch and J. Parry. London: Cambridge University Press.

———. 1989. "The Earth and the State: The Sources and Meanings of Money in Northern Potosí, Bolivia." In *Money and the Morality of Exchange,* ed. J. Parry and M. Bloch. New York: Cambridge University Press.

Haskett, Bert. 1935. "Early History of the Cattle Industry in Arizona." *Arizona Historical Review* 6 (4): 3–43.

Hastings, James, and Raymond Turner. 1965. *The Changing Mile.* Tucson: University of Arizona Press.

Hayden, Julian. 1987. "The Vikita Ceremony of the Papago." *Journal of the Southwest* 29 (3): 273–324.

Herzog, George. 1928. *Musical Styles in North America.* Proceedings of the Twenty-third International Congress of Americanists.

———. 1936. "A Comparison of Pueblo and Pima Musical Styles." *Journal of American Folklore* 49:281–417.

———. 1941. "Culture Change and Language: Shifts in the Pima Vocabulary." In *Language, Culture and Personality,* ed. Leslie Spier, A. Irving Howell, and Stanley Newman. Menasha, WI: Sapir Memorial Publication Fund.

Hill, Jane. 1992. "The Flower World of Old Uto-Aztecan." *Journal of Anthropological Research* 48 (2): 117–43.

———. 1996. *Languages on the Land: Toward an Anthropological Dialectology.* David Skomp Distinguished Lecture in Anthropology, Indiana University.

Hirschkind, Lynn. 1994. "Bedeviled Ethnography." *American Ethnologist* 21 (1): 201–4.

Hyde, Lewis. 1983. *The Gift.* New York: Random House.

Ingham, John. 1986. *Mary, Michael, and Lucifer: Folk Catholicism in Central Mexico.* Austin: University of Texas Press.

Jones, Richard. 1969. "An Analysis of Papago Communities, 1900–1920." Ph.D. diss., University of Arizona, Tucson.

Joseph, Alice, Rosamund Spicer, and Jane Chesky. 1949. *The Desert People.* Chicago: University of Chicago Press.

Kelly, William. 1974 [1963]. "The Papago Indians of Arizona." In *Papago Indians,* vol. 3, ed. David Agee Horr. New York: Garland Publishing.

Kennedy, John. 1978. *The Tarahumara of the Sierra Madre.* Arlington Heights, IL: AHM Publishing.

Kessell, John. 1969. "Father Ramon and the Big Debt: Tumacacori, 1821–1823." *New Mexico Historical Review* 44 (1): 53–72.

Kozak, David. 1991. "Dying Badly: Violent Death and Religious Change among the Tohono O'odham." *Omega* 23 (3): 210–17.

———. 1992. "Swallow Dizziness: The Laughter of Carnival and Kateri." *Wicazo Sa Review* 8 (2): 1–10.

———. 1994. "Reifying the Body through the Medicalization of Violent Death." *Human Organization* 53 (1): 48–54.

Kozak, David, and Camillus Lopez. 1991. "The Tohono O'odham Shrine Complex: Memorializing the Locations of Violent Mortality." *New York Folklore* 17 (1–2): 1–20.

Kroeber, A. L. 1976 [1925]. *Handbook of the Indians of California.* New York: Dover Publications.

Lamphere, Louise. 1983. "Southwest Ceremonialism." In *Handbook of North American Indians,* ed. W. C. Sturtevant. Vol. 10, *Southwest.* Washington, D.C.: Smithsonian Institution Press.

Lévi-Strauss, Claude. 1967 [1963]. *Structural Anthropology.* Garden City, New York: Anchor Books.
———. 1969 [1964]. *The Raw and the Cooked.* New York: Harper and Row.
———. 1995 [1978]. *Myth and Meaning.* New York: Schocken Books.
Manuel, Henry, Juliann Ramon, and Bernard Fontana. 1978. "Dressing for the Window: Papago Indians and Economic Development." In *American Indian Economic Development,* ed. Sam Stanley. Paris: Mouton Publishers.
Marcus, George. 1986. "Contemporary Problems of Ethnography in the Modern World System." In *Writing Culture: The Poetics and Politics of Writing Culture,* ed. J. Clifford and G. Marcus. Berkeley: University of California Press.
Marcus, George, and Michael Fischer. 1986. *Anthropology as Cultural Critique.* Chicago: University of Chicago Press.
McEachern, Charmaine, and Peter Mayer. 1986. "The Children of Bronze and the Children of Gold: The Apolitical Anthropology of the Peasant." *Social Analysis* 16:70–77.
Merrill, William. 1988. *Raramuri Souls.* Washington, D.C.: Smithsonian Institution Press.
Metzler, William. 1960. Untitled. Chapters concerning the economic potential of the Tohono O'odham Indians. Copy on file in the Arizona State Museum Library, University of Arizona, Tucson.
Miller, Wick. 1983. "Uto-Aztecan Languages." In *Handbook of North American Indians,* vol. 10, *Southwest,* ed. Alfonso Ortiz. Washington, D.C.: Smithsonian Institution Press.
Mintz, Sidney. 1996. *Tasting Food, Tasting Freedom.* Boston: Beacon Press.
Nash, June. 1972. "The Devil in Bolivia's Tin Mines." *Science and Society* 36:221–33.
———. 1979. *We Eat the Mines and the Mines Eat Us.* New York: Columbia University Press.
Ong, Walter. 1975. "The Writer's Audience Is Always a Fiction." *PLMA* 90:9–21.
Osgood, E. S. 1929. *The Day of the Cattlemen.* Minneapolis: University of Minnesota.
Painter, Muriel Thayer. 1988. *With Good Heart.* Tucson: University of Arizona Press.
Park, Douglas. 1982. "The Meanings of 'Audience.'" *College English* 44:247– 57.
Park, Willard Z. 1938. *Shamanism in Western North America.* Chicago: Northwestern University Press.

Parry, Jonathan. 1989. "On the Moral Perils of Money." In *Money and the Morality of Exchange,* ed. J. Parry and M. Bloch. Cambridge: Cambridge University Press.

Powers, William. 1992. "Translating the Untranslatable: The Place of the Vocable in Lakota Song." In *On the Translation of Native American Literatures,* ed. B. Swann. Washington, D.C.: Smithsonian Institution Press.

Roseberry, William. 1989. *Anthropologies and Histories: Essays in Culture, History, and Political Economy.* New Brunswick: Rutgers University Press.

Russell, Jeffrey. 1984. *Lucifer: The Devil in the Middle Ages.* Ithaca: Cornell University Press.

———. 1986. *Mephistopheles: The Devil in the Modern World.* Ithaca: Cornell University Press.

Russell, Frank. 1974 [1908]. *The Pima Indians.* Bureau of American Ethnology, Annual Report 26. Tucson: University of Arizona Press.

Said, Edward. 1982. "Opponents, Audiences, Constituencies, and Community." In *The Politics of Interpretation,* ed. W. J. T. Mitchell. Chicago: University of Chicago Press.

Sangren, Steven. 1988. "Rhetoric and the Authority of Ethnography: 'Postmodernism' and the Social Reproduction of Texts." *Current Anthropology* 29 (3): 405–35.

Schinhan, Jan Philip. 1937. "Die Musik der Papago und Yurok." Ph.D. diss., University of Vienna.

Schumm, S. and R. Hadley. 1957. "Arroyos and the Semiarid Cycle of Erosion." *American Journal of Science* 255 (3): 161–74.

Sheridan, Thomas. 1988. "Kino's Unforeseen Legacy: The Material Consequences of Missionization among the Northern Piman Indians of Arizona and Mexico." *Smoke Signal* 49–50:155–67. Tucson Corral of Westerners.

Silverblatt, Irene. 1980. "'The Universe Has Turned Inside Out . . . There Is No Justice of Us Here': Andean Women under Spanish Rule." In *Women and Colonization: Anthropological Perspectives,* ed. Moan Etienne and Eleanor Leacock. South Hadley, MA: Bergin & Garvey.

———. 1987. *Moon, Sun, and Witches: Gender Ideologies and Class in Inca and Colonial Peru.* Princeton: Princeton University Press.

Simpson, James. 1968. "Population Change in a Papago Community." M. A. thesis, University of Arizona, Tucson.

Spicer, Edward. 1962. *Cycles of Conquest.* Tucson: University of Arizona Press.

Spier, Leslie. 1978 [1933]. Yuman Tribes of the Gila River. New York: Dover Publications.

Sponsel, Leslie. 1992. "Information Asymmetry and the Democratization of Anthropology." *Human Organization* 51 (3): 299–301.

Sutton, David. 1991. "Is Anybody Out There?" *Critique of Anthropology* 11 (1): 91–104.

Taussig, Michael. 1980. *The Devil and Commodity Fetishism in South America.* Chapel Hill: University of North Carolina Press.

———. 1987. *Shamanism, Colonialism, and the Wildman: A Study in Terror and Healing.* Chicago: University of Chicago Press.

Underhill, Ruth. 1938a. *Papago Calendar Record.* University of New Mexico Bulletin No. 322, Anthropological Series 2 (5). Albuquerque: University of New Mexico Press.

———. 1938b. *Singing for Power.* Berkeley: University of California Press.

———. 1939. *Social Organization of the Papago Indians.* New York: Columbia University Press.

———. 1948. *Ceremonial Patterns in the Greater Southwest.* Seattle: University of Washington Press.

———. 1969 [1946]. *Papago Indian Religion.* New York: AMS Press.

Underhill, R., D. Bahr, B. Lopez, J. Pancho, and D. Lopez. 1979. *Rainhouse and Ocean: Speeches for the Papago Year.* Flagstaff: Museum of Northern Arizona Press.

U.S. Department of Commerce. 1975. *Operational Program for the Papago Livestock Facility.* Washington, D.C.: Economic Development Administration.

Vander, Judith. 1986. *Ghost Dance Songs and Religion of a Wind River Shoshone Woman.* Monograph Series in Ethnomusicology, No. 4. Los Angeles: University of California Press.

———. 1988. *Songprints: The Musical Experience of Five Shoshone Women.* Urbana: University of Illinois Press.

Waddell, Jack O. 1975. "For Individual Power and Social Credit: The Use of Alcohol among Tucson Papagos." *Human Organization* 34 (1): 9–15.

———. 1976. "The Place of the Cactus Wine Ritual in the Papago Indian Ecosystem." In *In the Realm of the Extra Human: Ideas and Actions,* ed. A. Bharati. The Hague: Moutin.

Wagoner, J. J. 1952. *History of the Cattle Industry in Southern Arizona, 1540–1940.* Tucson: University of Arizona Press.

Whitfield, Charles. 1970. Untitled. On file in the Arizona State Museum Library, University of Arizona, Tucson.

Williams, Richard. 1916. "The History of Livestock in Arizona." Arizona 6 (11).

Woodbury, R., and N. Woodbury. 1962. "A Study of Land Use on the Papago Reservation, Arizona." On file in the Arizona State Museum Library, University of Arizona, Tucson.

Xavier, Gwyneth. 1974 [1938]. "The Cattle Industry of the Southern Papago Districts with Some Information on the Cattle Industry as a Whole." In *Papago Indians,* vol. 1, ed. David Agee Horr. New York: Garland Publishing.

Index